AAM–1872

EC.AC
C64
753
1992

10 Ways To Build Enrollment In Your Early Childhood Program

Ellen Orton Montanari

BELMONT UNIVERSITY LIBRARY
CURRICULUM LAB

7236

CPG Publishing Company
Phoenix, Arizona

Published by: CPG Publishing Company
P.O. Box 50062 Phoenix, AZ 85076
1-800-578-5549

Copyright © 1992 by Ellen Orton Montanari

All rights reserved. No part of this publication may be reproduced or transmitted in any form or by any means, electronic or mechanical, including photocopy, or any information storage and retrieval system, without permission from the author.

Publisher's Cataloging in Publication Data
Montanari, Ellen Orton 101 Ways to Build Enrollment in Your Early Childhood Program / by Ellen Orton Montanari
1. Nursery schools – United States – Administration.
2. Day care centers – United States – Administration.
3. Marketing.

Library of Congress Catalog Card Number: 92-73368
ISBN: 1-882149-39-4

Cover design and graphics: Suzanne Nelson Company
Printed in the United States of America

This book is dedicated to all of the overworked and under-paid center directors in our country--who stay in their jobs because of their deep commitment to young children.

ACKNOWLEDGMENTS

This book would not have been possible without center directors from all over the country who have shared their ideas with me over the years. It is this spirit of sharing and collaboration that makes our field special!

A few people truly went above and beyond. Judy Crawford has shared many community marketing ideas with me over the years. Mary Jane Murdock was a great sounding board for me throughout this project. And Carolyn Zifka brings an infectious enthusiasm to her job, which (unbeknownst to her) inspired me to finish this book. Special thanks to Judy and Mary Jane, along with Sandy Foreman, Rene Manning and Cindy Olson for their careful and thoughtful review of my manuscript. Since all of them are current or former directors and owners of early childhood programs, their comments and suggestions were especially valuable.

When I've read acknowledgements in other books, I never understood why authors always mentioned how important their typists were. Well now I understand. Cheryl Ghormley's many suggestions and careful attention to detail were indispensable through the many drafts and revisions of the manuscript. And finally, taking my own advice, I asked a graphic artist to design the cover, graphics and layout. Suzanne Nelson's magic is evident throughout this book. I value and appreciate her creativity, patience and friendship.

Last but certainly not least, my thanks go to my husband, Dick. He is a college professor and has written textbooks in his field. He was a wonderful role model for me during this writing process. Without his support and optimism, I think this book might still be an idea floating around in my head.

TABLE OF CONTENTS

PREFACE

WHAT IS THIS BOOK?

This book is for directors and owners who want to *build* and *maintain* enrollment. It is designed primarily for centers that are operating in good locations and that offer quality programs with competitive prices. It is for directors and owners who may be intimidated by marketing, but would like to build enrollment. You will find that you do not have to be a marketing wizard or have a business degree to successfully build enrollment.

This book is designed with your budget in mind. Most early childhood programs I know don't have lots of money to invest in building enrollment. Most conscientious directors, owners and boards want to put their money into the children's program. That's why most of the ideas in this book don't cost much money. When they do cost, such as advertising, I give you tips on how to save money. Just look for the dollar signs.

WHAT THIS BOOK IS NOT

This is not a theoretical book. It is a practical, hands-on book that is full of tried and true ideas. It is for directors and owners who need help with marketing, but don't have time to take courses on marketing. These ideas have worked for child care centers across the country and I know many of them will work for you too.

This book does not contain an in-depth marketing plan. Instead, it includes a chapter about developing an action plan for building enrollment, which every center needs. If you have the time and resources to develop a detailed marketing plan, I encourage you to do so. This is especially important if you have several locations. Otherwise, take advantage of the simple, easy-to-use action plan in Chapter 5.

This is also not a marketing book designed for start-up operations. A new center will need a careful study of the area demographics to determine location and target market. While knowing demographics is important for all centers, this book is not designed to address those issues and others related to opening a new center. All start-up centers, however, will benefit from the ideas listed in this book, when they are supplemented with good market research.

You may notice that this book contains more than 101 ideas. I've actually listed 112 ideas. I found when I finished writing the book that I had more than 101 ideas. Rather than eliminate the extras, I decided to leave them for you. Just consider the extra ideas my gift to you!

HOW TO USE THIS BOOK

If you are the kind of reader who skips book introductions, don't skip this one. I know it is very tempting to skip these front pages and jump right into the "Ideas." Please read this section first! These five simple steps are the foundation on which to build enrollment in your center.

Step 1: Offer a quality program

All the marketing in the world is not going to help if you do not offer a quality program. As a matter of fact, a good marketing program, coupled with a mediocre early childhood program, will lead to *declining* enrollment. Why? Because a good marketing program means that people will learn sooner rather than later of your poor quality. Parents are smart consumers. You can bring them in with fast talking and glitzy marketing, but if the program is not good, they will not stay. And they will not refer their friends unless you offer a top quality program that meets their needs and their children's needs.

There are many good evaluation tools and checklists you can use to assess your program's quality. My favorites include the booklets published by NAEYC's National Academy of Early Childhood Programs and the *Early Childhood Environment Rating Scales* by Harms and Clifford. I encourage you to take a good look at your program and make any necessary changes before beginning a full-scale marketing program.

Step 2: Know your target market

You already know that it is important to know how many young children and families live in your area. However, you also need to know something about the families you want to attract to your program. They are known as your "target market" or "target audience."

You need to know some specific things about your target market. What benefits and features of an early childhood program appeal to them? What is the average size of these families? How old are the children? The parents? How educated are they? What is their family income? What do they do in their leisure time? What do they read? Do both parents work? Where do they live and work? Why would they want to come to your center? In addition you'll want to know about their buying habits, not just for child care but for all items. Are they apt to shop for quality or value? Is status and prestige important, or not so important? When you know the answers to these questions, you will know what types of written materials to develop for them, how to reach them when you promote your program and what to talk about when they call and visit.

You may want to change your existing target market. In other words, you may want to target a different type of parent for your program. For example, maybe you've been serving full-time children and want to attract half-day children. If you want to change your target market, you must be very careful. Many large companies have tried to change their target market and have failed miserably. Look at Sears, for instance. They decided they wanted to attract higher income families and were spectacularly unsuccessful. Not only did the families they targeted not change to Sears, but their middle income families left. Before changing your target market, you might want to consider hiring a child care marketing expert to see if it is feasible.

Step 3: Know what makes your program special (your competitive advantage)

What makes your program different from, and better than, all the other early childhood programs in your neighborhood? Why do parents come to your center rather than the one down the street? However you answer this — your staff/child ratios, extracurricular programs, price, or teacher qualifications —

becomes your competitive advantage. It should become the foundation of your marketing efforts.

To know what makes you special, you need to know your competition. Visit them, not just once, but periodically during the year. We all know how quickly a program can change, especially if there is a new director. Find out their prices, their services, the kinds of families they attract and what makes them special. How can you be better if you don't know who they are or what they are doing? When you know your competition, you know what you are doing better. This becomes the focus for everything you do to build enrollment.

Be careful how you define your competition. Don't limit yourself to other programs just like yours. For example, if you are in an all-day child care center, are family child care homes competing with you for children? How about the public schools? It is important to look at *all* programs that offer services to children in your area.

Step 4: Choose ideas from this book that fit your target market

Look through all the ideas in this book. Pick the ones you like and tailor them to meet your needs.

As you choose ideas, try to be consistent. The best way to understand consistency is through an example. Suppose your program is in an affluent part of town and you offer a quality early childhood program at above average prices. Your brochure should be on high quality paper, be typeset and deliver an upscale message. If you typed your brochure on your old Royal typewriter at home and ran it off at the local copy shop, you would not be giving your parents a consistent message. You're telling them that you offer an expensive, classy program, but your brochure says you are cost conscious. Whatever direction you choose, it is critical that you remain consistent and send clear messages to your potential families.

Look at your program. Who are the parents you want to attract? Does your brochure appeal to them? How about your logo? Are you advertising in places that reach your potential parents? Using the five P's will help you think consistently:

PRICE

PROGRAM

PLACE

PROMOTION

PARENTS

Are these consistent with each other in your early childhood program? Is your *price* consistent with what your *parents* can afford? Is your *program* something that *parents* want for their children? Is your *program* consistent with the needs of your neighborhood (*place*)? Are the messages in your *promotion* (such as advertising and public relations) consistent with your *program*? Remember: consistency is a major key to successfully reaching your target market.

Step 5: Develop a strategy for action

Make no mistake about it: a center without an action plan will not succeed in building enrollment. There are too many distractions in your job as director to keep you from building enrollment. It is too easy to become immersed in day-to-day tasks — helping a child adjust to her new classroom, hiring a new toddler teacher, refereeing a disagreement between your schoolage staff. It's too easy to say, "I'll work on marketing tomorrow."

An action plan doesn't have to be hard to develop or difficult to implement. I have outlined a simple, easy-to-use approach in Chapter 5. It will help you get your urgent job duties done and still leave time to build enrollment.

GETTING STARTED

Before you begin to promote your program in the community, get your "tools of the trade" in place. You'll find the investment in time and money worth it.

Many child care centers scrimp on stationery and business cards. But, I believe there are better places to save money. Most parents will see your business card, your brochure and your stationery long before they walk in your door. Every item with your imprint projects an image of your program. It means that parents will have a mental picture of your center before they see it.

Updating your image doesn't need to be expensive. I have included tips on saving money on stationery, brochures and business cards. While you may want to give your program a new face lift all at once, it is also acceptable to do it a little at a time. You can ask a graphic designer or graphic artist to design a new look for your center now, and purchase each piece a little at a time, as you run out of your current supplies of stationery and brochures.

Unless you have artistic talents, I strongly encourage you to use a graphic designer. I owned my company for several years before I broke down and had someone design a logo for me. When I saw what she did, and looked back on my old business cards and stationery, I was embarrassed. I should have done it years ago. And it didn't cost much. There are money-saving tips in this section on finding a graphic designer.

Look at your current business cards, stationery and brochures. Do they reflect the image you want to project? Are they designed to appeal to your target audience? If not, or if you're not sure, read on.

Come up with one sentence that describes your program to someone not in the early childhood field. To say, "we're a parent co-op," doesn't mean anything to someone who doesn't know what a parent co-op is. Avoid other early childhood jargon, such as "developmentally appropriate practices." While this means something to you, it doesn't mean anything to parents unless you take time to explain it. The one-line statement to describe your program needs:

- To say what makes you special
- To be brief
- To be concise
- To be clear

"We are a full-day educational child care program for working parents." "We are a half-day preschool program for three and four-year-olds." "Our full-day program is for children ages six weeks through six years and we focus on making learning fun."

Memorize it. Use it when talking to friends, associates and parents. Use that sentence everywhere. You can use it in your brochure, on flyers and all your materials. Practice saying it to others so they know exactly what you do.

2

Your logo is an important sales tool because it symbolizes your program. Logos can either be a picture (such as a teddy bear, a hot air balloon or a child) or a way of writing your center's name or a combination of both.

If you already have a logo, take a good look at it. Is it compatible with the image you want to project to your target market, both now and in the future? Is it compatible with your name? If it is in color, does it also look good in black and white?

If you do not have a logo, consider having one designed for you. If you have it done at the same time you have stationery, envelopes or a brochure designed, you will save money. It doesn't need to be expensive. Ask your local print shop to recommend someone. In Idea #3, there is more information about choosing a graphic designer.

TIP

Graphic designers will often charge you less if you are a nonprofit organization or if you are not in a hurry. If they can fit you between some of their larger clients, they may also charge less. If a parent is a graphic designer, he or she may be willing to trade reduced child care tuition for design work. You may have a parent who knows a graphics designer or whose company works with one. They may be able to negotiate deep discounts for you.

More ideas:

- Your new logo must be unique. It cannot look like your competitor's or you will confuse prospective parents.

- Use your logo everywhere. It should be on all your printed materials – brochures, business cards, signs, stationery, flyers, T-shirts, newsletter, van.

- As you develop new printed materials, use the same colors as you use in your logo. You want to associate your colors as well as your logo with your program. Coke uses the color red in its logo, American Express uses green and Kodak uses yellow. If they switched colors would the logos be the same?

IDEA **3** YOUR BROCHURE

Your brochure gives important information about your program to prospective parents. It will not sell parents on your school. Your staff, your program and you will sell parents. But you need to have a brochure to send them when they telephone. Your brochure is a tangible representation of your program to put into their hands. Give them another copy when they visit. Your brochure should include details about your center, such as hours and days of operation, your curriculum, special programs and transportation.

Have your brochure professionally produced. Its appearance is very important to parents since it is often the only tangible item about your program that they can take home. You offer a service. People cannot touch a service like they can touch a chair or a toy. What they can touch and take with them about your center is important. It must look professional and reflect the image you want your parents to see, not what you think is cute.

If your program is exclusive and expensive, your brochure must be too. Most programs, however, don't need an expensively produced brochure. If it is carefully worded and professional looking, it will be well received. Your brochure can be as simple as 8 1/2 x 11 paper folded in half or thirds. You will find that a three-fold (six panel) brochure fits into a #10 envelope and is the most versatile size for a brochure.

When you pick a designer for your brochure, ask your parents to recommend someone. You might be lucky and find that one of your parents is a graphic designer who will exchange design services for reduced tuition. If not, ask friends and colleagues for recommendations. You can often negotiate discounted services through your personal contacts. When you talk with designers, ask to see samples of their work. If you don't like anything you see, then interview others.

Talk about your budget. Ask how much they will charge. It doesn't have to be expensive to use a professional designer for your brochure. You can cut your costs by doing your homework ahead of time. Make an outline of what you want the brochure to say. Write out the information and put it where you think it should go in the brochure. This helps the designer understand how to organize and emphasize what you want to say in your brochure.

Decide if you want photos, line drawings or graphics. Ask the designer for printing cost information for each option. If you write your own copy, it is still a good idea to have a copywriter edit it. This is less expensive than having the copy written from scratch. You will be amazed at how great a good copywriter can make you sound. Your designer probably works with a copywriter or one of your parents may have the skill to do it.

TIP

You'll save money if you have your business cards, brochure and letterhead designed at the same time.

More tips:

- Use quality paper.

- Brochure colors must match your logo, business cards, stationery and signs. Be consistent!

- Plan to use your brochure for several years. Avoid rate information, the name of the director or other information that will date the brochure. You can provide up-to-date information on an insert to the brochure, on a flyer or on a handwritten note. Put the date on insert information that may change over time, such as tuition costs and availability in certain classrooms.

- Testimonials from satisfied parents are very powerful in a brochure. Solicit statements from satisfied parents. Use a quote from a letter you receive from a parent. Ask for permission. If the parent says yes, get permission in writing. This avoids future misunderstandings. Use the parent's full name and city. It is far more effective than using initials or first name only.

Don't hesitate to write testimonials for parents if they ask you to. This is common practice. When you give it to them, tell them to feel free to change the wording if they would like before they sign it.

TIP

Many directors want a full-color brochure, but can't afford it. If you don't need your brochures right away, talk with your local printer about being included on a "gang run." Here's how it works. You bring your camera-ready copy to the printer. When the printer receives a large order using a full-color layout, they run your job at the same time. You do not pay for cleaning up the presses after each color, which is why using several colors is expensive. You can have your full-color brochure at a price you can afford.

Business cards are your least expensive form of advertising. Use them everywhere. Always carry your business cards. I put mine in all my purses, my car and my briefcase. People ask me for cards in the oddest places. I've finally learned to always have one with me and it's really helped my business grow.

Give business cards to all your staff members and ask them to carry the cards all the time too. Put their names on the cards if you can afford it. Once you have paid for the set-up charges, it is really not expensive and it makes staff feel great. Remember, your teachers can be some of your best referral sources. If you cannot afford to put their names on the cards, give them business cards that look exactly like yours, but without a name or title. They can type or write in their names.

Let your business cards do double duty by letting them serve as mini brochures. You can use the back of the card for information or you can use a folding card. Include information such as your center's hours, your location, ages you serve and special programs (computer classes, swimming, gymnastics). Also include information about your "competitive advantage" – what makes you better than other early childhood programs in your area. Your competitive advantages can include low staff/child ratios, small group sizes, certified teachers, or accreditation by a professional organization.

More tips:

- Use standard size business cards. People like to keep all their business cards together. If yours doesn't fit in the stack, it might end up in the trash.

- Include your area code in your telephone number.

- Use quality card stock. Directors or owners who skimp on business card stock are forgetting about image. Remember the image you want to project about your program. Your business card stock can reflect that image.

- Consider getting magnetized versions of your business cards. People love magnets for their refrigerator doors. This keeps your center's name in front of prospective new families on a daily basis.

Along with all your printed materials, I recommend that your stationery be professionally designed. If you already have a logo, designing your stationery will be affordable. The designer at your local print shop can help at little or no cost, especially if you know how you want your stationery to look. Remember, you will save money if you have stationery, envelopes, logo and brochures designed at the same time.

Use the same colors in your stationery as in your logo and business cards. Many programs have two sets of stationery. One is printed in color for communication with parents. The other is printed in black and white for day-to-day correspondence (memos to staff, notes to suppliers). If you do this, *always, always, always* use your color stationery for personal notes to current parents and all correspondence with prospective parents. Your program's image is important and your stationery helps to convey that image.

Some directors do not have access to a computer or type-writer, while others prefer sending handwritten notes to parents. If you write by hand, consider purchasing stationery with faint lines to help you write a straight line. While parents appreciate a handwritten note, it reflects badly on you if your writing is not legible.

Your enrollment packet will either enhance or detract from your center's image. Remember, you are selling a service to parents, not a product. Manufacturers spend a lot of time and money on packaging for their products. Look at bottles for perfume and jewel cases for compact disks. Yet when you are marketing a service, you cannot package it. Or can you? While parents cannot carry your center home with them, they do carry home your enrollment packet. Your enrollment packet is part of your "package" and reflects your program's identity and image.

In general, the more upscale your program, the more attention you need to pay to the appearance of your enrollment packet. This doesn't mean it has to be expensive. You may want to have packets that are specially printed or embossed. If you purchase this type of packet, consider printing your philosophy statement inside the front cover. List all your services and special programs (such as computer, dance, summer program for schoolagers, swim lessons) to increase the possibility of parents using those services in the future.

You can buy plain packets to save money and have labels printed with your center's name, logo, address and phone number. If your computer printer is a laser printer or dot matrix with at least a 24-pin head, you can print the labels in your office.

Buy packets that match your logo colors with two pockets on the inside. If there is a cut-out for your business card, insert it there. If not, staple it to one of the pockets. If you purchase the plain packets, insert your philosophy statement and a listing of your services in front.

If you cannot afford printed labels and do not have a computer, staple your business card to the outside of each packet. No matter who your clientele, they will appreciate the professional appearance of a nicely packaged set of enrollment papers.

IDEA  **STICKERS**

Buy stickers from a print shop that say "Compliments of ABC Preschool." You will find dozens of uses for them. Put them on reprints of good parenting articles, on child care pamphlets (see Idea # 16), on advertising specialties that you give away at your center (Idea #38). It is a wonderful and inexpensive way to get your program's name out in the community.

Print the stickers with the name, address and telephone number of your school. Include your logo and a brief one sentence description of your program on the sticker. Use either your center's colors or purchase gold or silver stickers. It is important that the stickers be attractive. Remember, they also reflect your image. If they look cheap, parents will simply remove them.

IDEA  **POSTCARDS**

Use postcards as an easy, inexpensive way to communicate with current and prospective parents. They take less time to write and address than a letter and envelope and they take less postage. Have several hundred postcards printed on one side with your logo and return address. Leave the other side blank for personal notes. You can take a stack to the printer to print an announcement about an open house or other special event at the center. If you ever have someone design a newspaper or magazine ad, you can also reprint it on the cards and mail it to people on your mailing list. This gives you extra mileage for your advertising dollar.

Purchase name badges for all staff members. Have the name of your center and logo engraved on the badge. See your Yellow Pages under "Name Plates." Avoid using a hand-held label maker to imprint staff names. Your name badges must look professional. To save money, you can have a large quantity of badges printed with your center name and logo. The engraving company very often will keep the badges in the warehouse for you. As you have new employees join your staff, you can call the warehouse with the person's name and they will engrave the name for you. Having the person's name engraved generally costs under $7, which is well worth the extra advertising the badges will generate for you.

Ask staff members to wear their badges (and their accreditation ribbons, if your program is accredited) when they are working and when they are outside the center on center business. You should too. Wear it when you are on a field trip with the children. Wear it when you are shopping for the center. Have the van driver wear one when picking children up at public schools. You will be amazed at how many people will stop you and ask about your program.

IDEA **10** **FLYERS**

Flyers are useful when you want to distribute information to many people. They are less expensive than brochures, which you should save for prospective parents. Flyers should be bright and eye catching. A flyer's goal is to entice a prospective parent to call you, not to enroll in your program. Therefore, don't have a great deal of information on the flyer. Save that for your brochure.

Flyers need to look professional, but don't need to be professionally designed. Use a laser printer, along with clip art or graphics for illustrations. Ask your parents if any of them have desktop publishing capabilities.

Think about designing a half-page flyer so that you can print two flyers on one page. Use some of the extra money you save to put the flyers on brightly colored paper. Make sure your flyer colors are consistent with your logo colors.

TIP

You can give the impression of a two-color flyer for a fraction of the cost by using colored paper and the "ink of the day" from your local printer. Many printers have "free ink" days (for example, Monday is burgundy, Tuesday is brown, and so forth). On those days, the featured color costs the same as black ink.

Keep your message simple and quick to read. Add the word "free" and more people will pick one up. Depending upon your target audience and your pricing strategy, you might want to say "Special Offer" or "Valuable Coupon." Those words are powerful and increase the number of prospective parents you will reach.

If you have a professionally designed advertisement for your center, put it on a flyer and distribute it. This stretches your advertising dollars.

For ideas about where to distribute your flyers, see Idea #49.

IDEA **11** *MAILING LIST*

Your mailing list can be your most effective advertising tool. The people on the list already know you. They have already taken the first step and contacted you. Your mailing list also includes all the people you know who can refer families to your center.

How do you develop a mailing list? Take down the name and address of every person who calls your center or comes to visit. You can get this information from them by offering to send them your center's brochure. If they do not want your brochure, then offer to send them a pamphlet about how to choose quality child care. You can get copies from your local resource and referral agency or from the National Association for the Education of Young Children (NAEYC) in Washington, DC.

Even though parents on your list may have chosen a different program, or no program, keep them on your list. Maybe they will become unhappy with their existing child care arrangements. Maybe they didn't choose you because a job offer didn't come through, but now one has. Maybe a friend or neighbor needs a preschool. Whatever the reason, keep them on your mailing list. You may want to update and purge it based on a child's age. For example, if you don't take children over age four, you might want to eliminate families as their children reach their fifth birthday. You also may want to take them off your list after six months to one year from your last contact with them. Include the names and addresses of local businesses, real estate agents, elementary schools, pediatricians and human resource managers of companies in your area. These are all referral sources for your center.

How should you use your mailing list?

- Send invitations to parenting seminars.

- Send announcements about open houses that you host.

- Send your newsletter.

- Send notices of special promotions.

- Send a birthday card on a child's birthday.

Refer to the "Community Marketing" section of this book for more ideas.

IDEA 12 SIGNS

Your exterior signs must reflect the same theme as any advertising or printed material about your center. Your sign should use the same colors as your logo. Your logo should also appear on the sign. If people have seen your logo, even if it only registered unconsciously, or slogan (if you have one), they will recognize it again on your sign.

How does your sign look? Is it appealing? Is it clean and well maintained? A center in my neighborhood backs up to a busy thoroughfare. The owner takes advantage of that with a large sign easily seen by motorists. Since it is at the back of the school, however, the director doesn't see it on a day-to-day basis. The sign became weathered and the paint began peeling. It no longer reflects well on the school and gives passersby an inaccurate image of the program.

More tips to make your sign work hard for you:

- Put up the largest sign possible. Keep it simple. Use no more than six words, so passing motorists can read it easily.

- Use lettering that strongly contrasts with the sign's background color. For example, use light-colored lettering with a dark background color, or use dark lettering against a very light background.

- Use the same typeface throughout the sign's message to make your sign easier to read.

- Do not use handwritten signs. Have them professionally painted.

- Light up your sign so people can see it after dark.

- Put your telephone number on your sign.

2

PROMOTING YOUR PROGRAM

When you promote your program, you are letting people know what services you offer for families. Before families can enroll their children in your center, they have to know that you exist. There are many ways to promote your center. Here are the categories that make the most sense for early childhood programs:

- Community marketing
- Advertising
- Publicity
- Referrals

Community marketing is the work you do in the community that lets people know who you are and what your program is about.

Advertising is your paid promotions.

Publicity is media promotion that you receive for free.

Referrals are prospective families who come to your program on someone else's recommendations.

No one type of promotion can be effective by itself. For example, you cannot rely solely on referrals to build your enrollment. Your advertising dollars go farther when you couple them with community marketing. And publicity often works best for directors or owners who are also involved in community marketing.

As you select ideas in this section to promote your center, remember that the main purpose of promotion is to get prospective families to call you. Families will not enroll in your program based solely on your advertising or community marketing. But they will call. Choose ideas from this section that fit your program. Then get ready for the telephone to start ringing. The next chapter has telephone tips to help you answer those calls in a way to encourage more parents to visit your center.

COMMUNITY MARKETING

How do you define "community"? You might mean a three-mile radius around your center. If you live in a small town, you might mean the entire town. If you are near parents' work places, "community" may simply mean their office buildings. All of these are communities. You need to identify your community and use it as the focal point to market the services of your center.

Why promote your center in your community? We all know that "word of mouth" referrals are the primary way parents choose a child care center or preschool. Effective community marketing of your center begins with your existing parents who tell their friends about you. But think of other referrals you can get from neighbors and friends who know you have a great program. Think about pediatricians, dentists and other professionals who have heard of you and your center. Think about owners of children's stores and other shops near your center who have seen you and your children. Think about your local resource and referral agency or licensing specialist. These are all readily available "word of mouth" referral sources that can help make your center well-known in your community.

How can you help spread the "word"? Become involved in your community and people see your creativity and your competence. When you join a community organization, become active on a committee. Don't just attend general meetings to talk about your program. Let people see you working hard and they will also know that you work hard in your center. It is important, however, not to be seen as trying to hustle new business. The public needs to know that you are providing the information as a community service. When people perceive you are trying to hustle new business, they avoid you like the plague.

How can special events for families, parties, workshops and seminars spread the "word"? Special events are a great way to market your center. They attract your most committed enrolled families and this gives you the chance to strengthen your relationship with them. This not only means they are more likely to stay, but also more likely to refer others to you. Special events are perfect opportunities for your enrolled families to bring their friends to your center. It's a good way for new families to see your program in action.

Special events also attract your best potential families in the neighborhood. When new families attend your special events, be ready for them! Here are some ideas to help you prepare for these events:

- Always greet each one individually on arrival.

- Introduce new families to other families. Make sure they feel comfortable. They may not know anyone else at the event.

- Have brochures and business cards ready.

- Have a sign-in sheet. Add new visitors to your mailing list.

- If the special event is indoors, during the introductions briefly describe your program and services.

The more people who know you and your program, the more referrals you will receive. The key to promoting your program in the community is becoming known and recognized. That doesn't mean you need to spend lots of time outside your center. It also doesn't mean you need to become a celebrity. It simply means that when the Reese family moves into the neighborhood and asks if there is a good center nearby, their neighbors mention your center. Ms. Cardin decides her two-year-old has outgrown the babysitter, she remembers your name. It means if Mrs. Harker needs an after-school program, the receptionist at the local school gives her your name.

Marketing your program in the community often doesn't get immediate results. This can be frustrating. If you are writing a parenting column in your local newspaper or speaking in a college class, you will probably not get calls the same day for enrollments. It takes time to build your center's reputation in the community. But the long term rewards are worth the time and effort.

How do you market your center in your community? The ideas that follow have worked for me and for other directors. They can work for you as well.

Write a community-based newsletter. Let your staff write an in-house newsletter that you distribute to your families. The community newsletter that you write will go outside your center.

The goal of this newsletter is to keep your center's name in front of prospective families. Those who receive your newsletter will probably not need child care when they get it. But when they do need your services, or when a friend does, they will think of your center first.

What should be in this newsletter? Include parenting tips, timely articles on child care issues, book reviews, ideas for activities that parents can do at home with their children, and announcements of new offerings at your center. Profile a different staff member in each issue. Give a brief summary of past and upcoming events in your center. Each issue should contain a brief description of your program and services, emphasizing what makes you different from other early childhood programs.

Who should receive this newsletter? Your existing families. Everyone on your waiting list. People who have called or visited your program, but did not enroll. Local shops, pediatricians, and business owners in your area. Be creative!

The newsletter doesn't need to be fancy, but it does have to look professional. If one of your parents has access to desktop publishing or a good computer and laser printer, enlist their services. You might be able to trade child care tuition for help in layout and design. Watch for typos, misspellings and poor grammar. Let someone else read and edit it before it goes out.

Send out your newsletter at least quarterly. Try it for at least two years, then evaluate its effectiveness. You might want to consider purchasing a semi-customized newsletter. Some companies have developed generic newsletters with articles about children's issues, and leave space for you to add specific information about your center. This may be more cost-effective for you.

Prospective parents don't like open houses because they expect you to pressure them to enroll their children. Bring in speakers on popular parenting topics instead. Invite enrolled parents and encourage them to bring friends. Distribute flyers in your neighborhood and send special invitations to everyone on your newsletter mailing list.

Successful topics:

- Biting
- Discipline problems
- Is my child ready for school?
- Teaching my child to read
- Tantrums
- Sibling rivalry
- Toilet training

With the "ready for school" and "ready to read" topics, you can address developmentally appropriate practices, which helps parents understand why workbooks and flash cards are not the best way to learn to read.

Offer free or low-cost babysitting during the seminars. Use your best teachers to supervise the caregiving to showcase their talents.

By hosting these seminars, your center becomes known as a resource in the neighborhood. Have brochures and business cards to distribute to all who attend. Don't forget to get everyone's name and address and put them on your mailing list. For more information on using your mailing list effectively, see Idea #11.

Offer to write a regular parenting column in your local or community newspaper. This is especially effective in smaller neighborhood newspapers. As readers see your name and your center's, they will identify you as an expert. When it's time to choose a child care program, they will call you first.

If you're not secure about your writing skills, consider working with an editor or ghostwriter. You can get names from your local university or from *Writer's Digest*, a magazine for writers.

It is important not to sell your program or center in your column. The purpose of the column is to educate parents. Don't worry, your expertise will come through loud and clear! Do mention the name and address of your center, along with a concise, one-line description of your program in the brief biography, called a "bio," at the end of your column.

If there is a large corporation in your community, send your column to them for their employee newsletter. You can also send child care or parenting articles by other authors. Ask the authors or publication for reprint permission. They will be glad to comply as long as you give them a credit line.

TIP

Whether you are writing an article, appearing at a meeting in the community or hosting a special event, always give a brief description of your center, its services and what makes your program special. If you are talking, keep it to fifteen seconds, but write it out in advance. If you are writing an article, include a brief statement at the end of the article that gives your name and title, your center's name, address and telephone. Then add a sentence about your services. The publication may include this information in a small box after the article, but it certainly won't appear if you don't write it at all.

Pamphlets about child care and parenting are available from a number of local and national sources. I like the ones available through NAEYC. They are professional and very affordable. At this printing, the cost was only $10 for 100 copies. When you hand them out to families in your area, you are seen as an expert and resource for families. These pamphlets are very nonthreatening to families, because you don't sell anything with them. You are simply giving useful information to parents. Attach your "Compliments of . . . " sticker to each pamphlet (see Idea #7).

Where can you distribute these pamphlets? Refer to the possibilities listed in Idea #49. You will certainly think up your own as well.

Organize a party at your center on Halloween night. Many parents are afraid to let their children go out into the neighborhood to trick or treat. A Halloween party is a great alternative and it is a good opportunity for families in your area to see your school. Invite all your enrolled families, as well as the rest of your community through your newsletter, flyers or postcards. You may want to put an age limit on children ("children between the ages of two and ten are cordially invited . . . "). Ask for an RSVP. You need to know how many children are planning to come and their ages. Have plenty of refreshments, games and activities ready for all ages. Have your staff and their friends come in to help with the children's activities. You will need plenty of help, since many parents will want to socialize with other parents. This is a good opportunity for you to show how well you organize activities.

Assign key staff members to help new families get acquainted. Encourage everyone to get involved in the activities. Your goal is to make everyone feel at home. Have brochures ready at your sign-in table. Remember to add new families to your ongoing mailing list.

IDEA **18** ◄ *HOT AIR BALLOONS*

Families love hot air balloons. One of our most successful neighborhood parties centered on one. A parent who owned a hot air balloon gave children and their parents tethered balloon rides. We distributed notices in the neighborhood ("Everything's ballooning but our rates!"). We offered food, tours of the center, games and activities on the playground, and of course, balloon rides. We were only charged for propane and added insurance for the day, but we would have gladly paid more, given the great exposure we received that day in the neighborhood.

Secretaries and receptionists in local elementary schools greatly influence parents' child care choices. Parents often ask elementary school receptionists about child care for both preschool and after-school care. Make it a point to keep in touch with school receptionists in your area on a regular basis. Try some of these suggestions:

- Every August, take a handful of pencils with your program's name, address and phone number engraved on them to school receptionists. Your center's name is never far from their fingertips!

- Take a basket of apples for school secretaries and receptionists in the fall and near the end of the school year (if you offer summer programs). Refill the basket once a week for four or five weeks.

- Give mugs engraved with your center's name, logo, address and telephone number to school secretaries.

- If you offer transportation for schoolagers, there may be times when you cannot find a child after school who is supposed to ride with you. Send a note to the principal when the school office staff helps you find the child and let the principal know how helpful the staff was.

Rapport with all school professionals is important for future referrals. Try these ideas:

- Meet with the K-3 curriculum specialist, if there is one. Otherwise, meet with kindergarten teachers. Ask how they would like you to prepare children for their school.

- Offer a discount or free registration fee to schools during kindergarten registration. PTOs or PTAs are often interested when you offer discount certificates.

- Meet with principals of schools in your area just to establish rapport. Take a copy of your curriculum guidelines, your brochure and a business card.

IDEA 20 **HOST EVENING CLASSES**

If your liability insurance allows it, offer to host evening classes in Jazzercise, aerobics, CPR or first aid. Offer your center as a meeting place for clubs or groups. You can sometimes charge a small rental fee to cover utility and maintenance costs. Have flyers or brochures available in the room where people meet, along with your current newsletter. While the people coming to your center may not have children of their own, they have friends or relatives who may someday need child care.

IDEA 21 **DIAPER SERVICES**

If you offer infant or toddler care, ask diaper services to distribute your brochures to families in your neighborhood. Develop a small packet that includes your brochure, a list of safe, easy-to-make baby toys and a small rattle or other gift. Include a coupon for a free gift or tuition discount to encourage new parents to visit your center.

Consider joining business networking groups in your immediate area. The main purpose of networking is to trade information on business leads. Some groups are better than others, so it pays to be selective. Call existing members to ask why they attend meetings and how long they have belonged to the group. Then try a few groups for a trial period of at least six months. You will have the opportunity to stand up and give a short "pitch" about your center. Prepare both a ten-minute and a fifteen-to-twenty-second presentation about your program, services and benefits. Write the short description on a card that you carry with you. You will always be ready to stand up and talk about your program. Bring lots of business cards and brochures or flyers about your center. If you prepare a ten-minute presentation, bring photographs to pass around. Our profession lends itself well to the old saying, "One picture is worth a thousand words."

At the beginning of the school year, be a guest on a local radio talk show. Offer to talk to listeners about how to choose quality child care for young children. During the show, make sure you reference your program by making statements like, "Here's what we do at ABC Preschool," or "At ABC Preschool here's what we encourage parents to look for when they visit our school." You are not directly selling your program, but you are making sure that the listeners know your center's name. There are two benefits to a radio show. First, you are recognized in the community as an expert. Parents prefer their children to be cared for by experts. Second, you are getting your school's name into the community at no cost to you. This type of radio advertising would cost you thousands of dollars if you had to pay for it.

Avoid controversial radio talk shows. Ask the host if there will be any other guests with you on the show. As an owner or director of an early childhood program, you should not be debating the pros and cons of child care licensing, federal money for child care or whether or not mothers should work. I have talked to countless directors who thought they could handle the challenge. Instead they ended up feeling miserable about their treatment by the talk show host, the other guest and the listening audience. If your goal is to use talk shows as a way to showcase your child care expertise and obtain positive publicity for your program, stick to noncontroversial topics.

IDEA **24** **TELEVISION**

Call your local television station to see if they would be interested in doing a feature for parents on quality child care. Start with a cable station if you feel nervous about approaching a local network station. They all do some type of community programming and programs for young families are popular. How to discipline your child is another favorite topic. Offer to help research the topic and be a local resource. As a caution, only talk about issues about which you are knowledgeable.

IDEA **25** **ALUMNI NEWSLETTER**

Here is an unusual idea for promoting your program. If your center is located in the same community where you went to college, submit an article to your alumni newsletter. Ask for a couple of back issues to see what kind of articles they publish. Some newsletters are very serious, while others prefer silly or off-beat articles. Include a description of your business and its location in your article. Enclose a black and white photograph of you with children from your center, along with an appropriate caption.

IDEA **26** *PACKETS TO PARENTS OF NEWBORNS*

If you offer an infant program, send a packet to parents of babies born at your local hospital. You can include a small gift, a brochure about how to choose infant care, a flyer about easy-to-make baby toys and, of course, your brochure and an invitation to visit your center.

One Jewish early childhood program director told me that they look for "Jewish names" in the newspaper and send T-shirts that say "Class of ——" on the front, along with a coupon for their parent/infant class. This idea has been resoundingly successful for them. While you may not have a Jewish program, a variation of this idea may work for you. You can also purchase mailing lists of parents with new babies in your neighborhood. For hints about purchasing mailing lists, see Idea #48.

IDEA **27** *MOVING COMPANIES*

Make arrangements with local moving companies to provide free child care on moving day or week. Parents are eternally grateful for this service and often sign up with your center. They also become terrific referral sources for you.

IDEA 28 LOST CHILD BOOTH

Operate a booth for lost children at local events, like a major mall opening, Renaissance fair or children's fair. Make sure they have a public address system available. Confirm that either your center or the event has insurance to cover your activities. Arrange to have your booth located in a prominent spot. Use a large banner that includes your center's name.

Write a brief statement for periodic announcement, such as "ABC Preschool is sponsoring a booth for lost children. It is located in the southwest corner next to the entrance. If you lose your child, please come by the ABC Preschool booth." Even if families do not lose their children, they hear your name repeated over and over. Ask the event sponsor if you can hand out free gifts. If so, add this line to your announcement: "Even if you haven't lost your child, visit our booth before you leave and pick up your free gift." A good and inexpensive gift is a small plastic bag of homemade playdough, tied with a ribbon and your business card.

IDEA 29 COLLEGE CLASSES

If the community college or university near your center offers early childhood or parenting courses, get to know the instructors. Offer to attend their classes as a guest speaker. Pick a topic that is compatible with the course. NAEYC accreditation (if your program is accredited), toddler behavior or state licensing of child care centers are all good topics. As part of your introduction, describe your center's location, the ages you serve, and your program. I have received many new parents and employees from speaking to classes.

IDEA 30   HOST A RECEPTION

If your local professional organization brings in a noted speaker as a keynoter, offer to host a reception at your center. Even if the person is well-known, don't be bashful about offering. There is a good chance no one made arrangements for the speaker to spend time in a child care center. Invite parents, people on your mailing list and friends to the reception. Offer refreshments. Have a sign-in sheet to add new people to your mailing list. Provide names tags. Have plenty of brochures on the sign-in table.

In your welcoming statement, mention the name of your program, along with your one- sentence statement about your services (see Idea #1).

IDEA 31   DECEMBER ENROLLMENT

Do you have trouble with decreased enrollment during December? Offer child care on Saturdays or stay open either one or two nights a week. Advertise it as a service to your existing families so they can do their holiday shopping. Consider offering the service to friends of your existing families too. Remember, December is a month when many parents change their child care arrangements. This is a great opportunity to introduce new families to your center.

ADVERTISING

On first thought, advertising spells "big bucks." It is possible to spend lots of money on advertising, but it's not necessary. It's important, though, to spend some money. You cannot rely solely on word-of-mouth referrals for the success of your center. Referrals will maintain your enrollment levels, but won't build them quickly. Advertising can.

The following tips will guide you in the use of your advertising dollars and also keep you within your budget.

- Develop an advertising budget. Decide in advance how much money you can afford to spend. Some programs spend a percentage of their revenue. Others spend or "invest," as some directors say, a certain dollar amount per child for advertising.

- Plan carefully. Don't sign up with every advertising sales person who calls or visits you at your center.

- Decide who you want to reach with your advertising. Target your market. What do they read? Where do they shop? Choose the advertising techniques and the media that appeal to your target families.

- Emphasize your competitive advantage in your ads. Your competitive advantage may be the convenience of your location or hours, your educational program or your staff. Phrase your competitive advantage in your customers' terms, which means you'll focus on benefits, not features. Refer to Idea #75 for information about benefits and features.

- The goal of advertising is to have people remember your program. Use your logo in every ad. Use more than one form of advertising to get your message to parents. When you see what type of advertising works for you, stay with it. Repeat the ad and avoid skipping around. Parents remember your program when they see or hear your advertising repeatedly.

- Your ads must look professional, but don't have to be slick or expensive. Parents want their money going into the program, not into expensive advertising.

- Last, but certainly not least, track all your advertising. When parents call your program, ask them how they heard about you. When they enroll, ask again. Keep track of the ads that stimulate calls and use them again. It is important to know which ads are working for you, so that your budget is spent wisely.

What is the key advantage of advertising? Unlike publicity, you control the message that goes out to parents. The key disadvantage of advertising is that it can be expensive. Some of the advertising ideas in this section are more expensive than others. To help make them more affordable, I have included tips on how to save money when using costly advertising media. While you may decide many are out of your budget's reach, you should at least be aware of the different types. This will help you make educated decisions about your marketing dollars.

Next to word-of-mouth referrals, the Yellow Pages are the most frequent source parents use to find child care. While many parents use the Yellow Pages, few will say so. Perhaps parents feel it is okay to say they looked in the Yellow Pages to find a carpet cleaner, but not a program for their child. Nevertheless, most parents use a number of sources and do rely on the Yellow Pages for their first contact. Yellow Pages advertising is expensive, so it pays for you to think carefully about how and where you place your advertisement.

Like all your printed advertisements, don't have the Yellow Pages sales rep design your ad. They are not designers. It is worth the money to have a professional design your ad, since you will be able to use it over and over again. I have tried it both ways. I became a true believer after my professionally designed ad dramatically increased my telephone inquiries.

Use the Yellow Pages for detailed information to prospective families. Tell them your hours, ages you serve, special programs and if you are accredited. By all means, tell them what makes your program special. If it's your terrific staff/child ratios, tell them. If it's your educational program, or your park-like playground, your computers or your warm, loving, credentialed staff, tell them.

Maintain a personal tone in your ad. Looking for a program for children is an emotional decision for parents. The more your ad can put them at ease and make them feel your program is the best place for their child, the more calls you will receive.

Look at other centers' ads. What do you like? What don't you like? What do you think would appeal to your prospective parents? Write down your ideas and thoughts and take them to a graphic designer or professional copywriter.

You can choose a display ad or an in-column ad. In-column ads are less expensive and make lots of sense if the name of your center is near the beginning of the alphabet. For a little extra money, you can sometimes add color to make your in-column ad stand out. If no one else is using color, your in-column ad will stand out more than an expensive display ad.

Be careful about competitive Yellow Pages directories. Most of the competing directories are not effective. While their ads are less expensive, your potential customers may not be using that directory. How can you tell? Call child care centers or other related businesses that are listed in the competing directory to ask if they have benefitted from their listing in the directory.

Track your customers to see how many of them found you through the Yellow Pages. I have done this by attaching a small colored sheet of paper to enrollment papers, asking parents how they found us. I gave them several choices to check off, such as friend, flyer, door hanger, advertisement or Yellow Pages. I include a category called "other" for write-in options.

You can list your center under "child care" or "private schools" in the Yellow Pages. The effectiveness of the private school listing varies from community to community. Look at both sections in your Yellow Pages. If most programs like yours put their large display ads and bold listings in one category, it is likely to be the category used most frequently by prospective families. If you are uncertain, try listing in both places, using different telephone numbers in each ad. By tracking the number of inquiries you receive on different phone lines, you can determine which ad is most effective. If you are unable to do this, you can also ask families which ad they used to find you when they enroll. This may seem like extra work, but Yellow Pages advertising is expensive. If an ad is not working for you, it is important to know about it. You can either change or eliminate the ad before you spend too many advertising dollars on ineffective advertising.

Even though Yellow Pages advertising is expensive, don't rely on it as your only advertising outlet. It is only one of many avenues to explore to promote your program.

Use newspaper advertising carefully. It is expensive and doesn't always reach your target market of prospective new families. This is especially true if you advertise in larger metropolitan newspapers. These newspapers reach far beyond your neighborhood, which means you're paying to reach readers who aren't part of your target market.

If you live in a large city, local and neighborhood newspapers work best, since your parents generally come from your center's immediate neighborhood. In addition, many large metropolitan newspapers have regional editions or sections. With your target group of parents in mind, it might make sense to advertise in the regional sections or editions of large newspapers, rather than in the main edition.

If you decide to try newspaper advertising, have a graphic artist design your ad. Don't let the newspaper's advertising department do it for you.

TIP

If you use a graphic designer, ask for an ad to use in several media, such as newspapers, newsletters or magazines. Use this advertisement again and again. You only pay once for a graphic designer. You can also track the effectiveness of your ads.

Include a "window" in your advertisement so you can insert special offers, such as one free week. If you want people to respond immediately to your advertisement, it is important to offer something, such as a free week, free registration fee or one-half off. Put an expiration date on the coupon to give your ad a sense of urgency.

If you are going to use newspaper advertising, give your advertisement time to work. Run your ad in the same place in the newspaper each week. Run it for at least three months in a row. Research shows that people need to see an ad a number of times before they remember it. Newspaper advertisements are generally most effective if they are on the right side, near the right margin, above the fold.

A newspaper insert is a flyer that is inserted into individual newspapers. It can be a cost- effective way to advertise in your local or neighborhood newspaper. You can usually specify the neighborhoods where you would like the flyer to be distributed, allowing you to target neighborhoods very carefully.

In most instances, you provide copies of the flyer and the newspaper charges you to insert them.

Inserts work very well with local newspapers, as long as there aren't too many of them. Inserts lose their impact when readers see them in every edition. Make sure yours is colorful and eye-catching.

Include a coupon for a free week or a free gift for stopping by. That way you can judge the effectiveness of the insert.

Although classified advertisements are less expensive than display ads, you must use them with care. If your families are high income, they may not want to see their child's school in the want ads.

If you decide that classified ads will work for you, choose publications that your prospective parents read. Try parenting magazines, community newspapers and neighborhood newsletters.

Don't make the mistake of running a short ad just to save money. Don't use abbreviations. Use complete sentences. Describe your services. Make it personal.

You will need to run a classified ad more than once before you can judge its effectiveness. Give it several weeks or months, depending on whether it is a weekly or monthly publication. If the classified ad is successful, you may want to try a display ad in the same publication to see if it draws more calls.

When is the best time to run classified ads? Try before, during and slightly after key enrollment periods: fall, New Year, and late spring if you offer a summer program.

Newspapers are read and thrown away each day. Magazines have a longer shelf life, which means your ad is seen for months. Magazine ads are particularly good if your market is affluent. If your advertising budget includes an investment in magazine ads, use them only if you believe they will make your phone ring.

Targeted, local magazines work best. Look for publications your parents are likely to read. Spend some time in the library with *Standard Rate and Data Service*, a publication that tells you the circulation of magazines, who their audiences are and how much their ads cost.

Target key enrollment times for running ads and run them more than once. Track your advertisement carefully to see how many responses you receive.

Have the ad professionally designed. This is not a time for homemade art. I know I sound like a broken record, but don't let the magazine's art department design your ad. You will do better with your own designer.

Once your ad appears in a magazine, stretch your advertising dollar further and have reprints made. You can use these for flyers. Include a banner on the flyer saying, "As seen in XYZ Magazine" if the magazine is a prestigious one. Distribute the flyers throughout your neighborhood (see Idea #49). Send them out to people on your mailing list. Give them to prospective parents when they visit your center. As with other printed advertisements, this gives you multiple uses of one ad.

TIP

Do not pay full rates. Get a copy of the magazine's rate card. These full rates are where you begin to bargain. Call up the magazine's advertising department and tell them you are interested in advertising in their publication, but are on a limited budget. Let them know you are interested in purchasing unsold ad space at the last minute at reduced rates. Have a copy of a magazine ad ready to go and wait for their call. If you use this method, you will save lots of money, but it can cause problems. You cannot target your key enrollment times and usually cannot run back-to-back ads, unless there is unsold space in back-to-back issues. This is a great way, though, to get magazine exposure for little money.

For most centers, radio and television advertising are not practical or cost-effective. This type of advertising works best if you have several locations or have a very large school that draws families from all over the city.

If your organization is large enough or if you decide you would like to try radio advertising, here are some tips:

Radio is considered a "low impact" marketing tool, which means you need to repeat your message over and over again to be effective. Run the ad several times a day, several days a week and at least three weeks out of every four.

Learn the demographics of your target parents. Where do they live? What do they do in their spare time? How much money do they make? Do both parents work? What radio stations do they listen to and when? Do they listen on the way to work? Contact radio stations and ask a sales representative about the demographics of the station's listening audience. They can also tell you the audience size.

If you decide that radio advertising is for you, consider having a radio personality do the ad for you. Ask the announcer to come to your center for a tour or to one of your special events. Provide an outline of what the ad should cover. The person then "ad-libs" a personal ad based on the visit and your outline. This works best if the announcer is a popular personality.

TIP

A station's rate card (the cost of advertising) is only a place to start negotiating. Make them an offer!

Advertising specialties are inexpensive items on which you imprint your center's name, address, telephone number and logo. They are designed for your enrolled families, as well as prospective ones. Consider with care how and why you will distribute them. Select a specialty that fits early childhood programs. A key chain, for example, does not have much to do with young children, but a child growth poster does. You might want to use coffee mugs for the secretaries and receptionists at your local elementary schools (where your schoolagers attend) or for your local resource and referral specialists. One program used plastic magnets in the shape of a house and imprinted its name, logo, address and telephone number. These magnets always end up on refrigerator doors, even if parents decide not to use your program. If they do change their minds, your name is right in front of them. Other appropriate advertising specialties include children's visors or logo shoe strings.

Advertising specialties reflect your center, so choose quality items. Always see a sample before buying. You can find companies that offer advertising specialties in the Yellow Pages.

Calendars are used by many businesses to keep the name of their company in front of customers all year. While this may not be important for most early childhood programs, it might make sense for some of you. For example, it is difficult to reach new families when your center is located near the work place. Your parents live all over the city or town, which makes local advertising ideas expensive to implement. If you give desk or wall calendars to your families to use at work, your center's name will be seen by everyone who walks into your parents' work areas.

You can order calendars from office supply or advertising specialty companies. The key here is to get attractive calendars. Everyone throws ugly, cheap calendars away. Since we are in the early childhood field, use children or families as the theme. If you want parents to use them in the work place, select calendars carefully. Before you order, ask some of your parents which ones they like best. Your taste may be different from that of your target audience.

Consider advertising on grocery store carts. Most stores now have frames mounted to their carts for businesses to insert small cards advertising their services.

Know your target audience. An ad for your center on a shopping cart may seem too commercial for your parents.

If you like this idea, select a store near your center where many of your target families shop. Talk to the store manager about rates. If you decide to advertise, have the signs professionally designed and printed. The store manager can usually give you a referral to get the cards printed.

You usually can have your ad on the inside or outside of the cart. Place your ad on the inside, so the customer sees it while pushing the cart.

IDEA **41** **YOUR VAN**

If your program owns a van, you have a built-in form of advertising. Does your van have a sign painted on it? It should include your center's name, logo, address (with major cross streets listed) and telephone number. Put it on the side and back panels, with your telephone number featured prominently. You might also want to list the ages you serve and your competitive advantage. This makes your van a moving billboard. Since your program's image in the community is important, have the van signs painted by a professional.

Once your van sign is painted, keep the van clean, both inside and outside. Your van is often a parent's first introduction to your program. It is your on-the-go, roving advertisement. Use it to your best advantage.

If your local zoning laws allows them, use temporary banners on your building. Banners have special impact if your center is on a busy street or commuter route. Display eye-catching announcements, such as "Enroll in our summer program now," "Now enrolling in our toddler program," or "Now offering computer classes for kids." Always list your telephone number.

Passing motorists need to easily read your sign. Hang the sign as high as possible. The higher it is, the more visible it is. Use very large letters. The larger they are, the easier it is to read the sign from a distance.

Personalize the message. Try "Enroll your preschool child now," rather than "Preschool Enrollment." Give immediacy to your message with phrases like, "Enroll your child today." Announce a giveaway or special savings with, "Free registration" or "Special savings this week." Give people a reason to stop.

Avoid handwritten banners or homemade banners with stencils. If you use homemade banners, have them painted by an artist.

Contact city hall to check on banner ordinances. Some cities and towns don't allow banners and others restrict their usage.

Have T-shirts imprinted with your center's name, logo and address. There are several ways to use T-shirts to advertise your program. You can give free T-shirts to children who enroll in your summer program. You can offer children's T-shirts for sale. You can give a free T-shirt to children when they first enter the program so children can wear them every time they go on a field trip. Keep extras in the center for those children who forget theirs. However you decide to do it, children who wear your program's imprinted T-shirts are walking billboards for your program.

Some programs also order nice golf shirts with the center's name, logo and address for staff members. You might decide to let them wear the shirts whenever they wish, or you can use them as part of your center's uniform. Programs that use a shirt as part of a uniform generally buy each staff member three or four shirts and sell additional ones to them at cost. The employees can wear the shirts with slacks, shorts or casual skirts. It is a good way to have a professional look without taxing employees' pocketbooks.

IDEA **BUTTONS**

You can use buttons the same way you use T-shirts. Think about buttons that say "I'm from ABC Preschool" with your logo, address and phone number for children to wear on field trips. By the way, you should never have children's names pinned on their shirts on a field trip. It is too easy for a stranger to call out, "Johnny, come here. Your mommy wants to see you." Only list the center's name and phone number.

You can also give buttons to your teachers to wear if you have a special event coming up. The buttons can say, "We're planning a Super Summer at ABC Preschool," or "Ask me about our new infant program." It's corny, but it works!

IDEA **BULLETIN BOARD SIGNS**

Bulletin board signs in nearby businesses often attract parents from your neighborhood. Make a small pocket for your business cards. Never use tear-offs on your bulletin board flyers. It doesn't look professional. To save money, use the same flyer that you developed for other purposes, without the coupon if desired. (See Ideas #10 and #49.)

Door hangers are advertisements that are hung on front door knobs of homes in your area. They work especially well for neighborhood businesses like preschools and child care centers. You can deliver them solely to key neighborhoods near your center. I like door hangers for grand openings, special events or a new service, like infant care or new hours.

Door hangers can be a good advertising tool under certain conditions: they must be professionally designed, they must include a special offer and they must be distributed by a professional company or civic group you can trust.

Door hangers need to be eye-catching. People have so many things hung on their doors, they generally throw them away before looking at them. A professional designer can help here. I have found their services more than pay for themselves by the number of responses I have received from unusual door hangers.

Don't put them in plastic bags that hang on the door. They make the door hanger too easy to toss out without reading. Have a die cut door hanger. I think it's worth it.

Door hangers are more successful when you offer a coupon or a free gift. For a special event, you can offer free food or entertainment. In the case of a seminar, offer free babysitting for children.

There are services that will hang them for you. Check the company out carefully. Ask them for references. Call the references and ask about the company's reliability and the attire of the people who hang the flyers. You want distributors who are neat, clean and project a positive image for your center.

TIP

Call your local Boy or Girl Scout Troop, children's soccer team or high school club to distribute your door hangers. Both of you benefit. You have your door hangers distributed for a reasonable price and have built some good will in your neighborhood. They have extra money in their coffers for a special project. I recommend that you add a line on your hanger that credits the distributors that says, "This flyer was delivered to your home by the Miramesa Girls Soccer League."

There are newspapers and periodicals that are networking publications. If you write a column, called an "advertorial," for the periodical, you get free advertising space. In some networking publications, you pay to write a column that also includes a display ad. It is an interesting way to get your name in the public eye with little or no investment. If you decide to use this idea, choose the publication carefully. Find out how many people receive it, who the readers are and where they are located. Are they people who are likely to use your center or refer other families to it?

Include your picture in the paper, along with your title and the name of your program. People will identify you as an expert. When they need child care, they will think of you first.

Direct mail can work well for neighborhood service businesses. With a good mailing list, you can use direct mail to pinpoint your target audience accurately. This is especially important with a neighborhood business like yours.

On the other hand, direct mail can be costly. With an inaccurate mailing list, it can be disastrously expensive. Direct mail is only as good as its mailing list.

If you decide that direct mail advertising will work for your program, start collecting direct mail pieces that you receive. Collect both those you like and dislike. Show the ones you like to some of your favorite parents to see how they react. Based on their responses, design a flyer. For best results, include a coupon for a discount or free gift.

When choosing a company to provide your mailing list, ask for references. If possible, the references should be service firms in your area. Ask mailing list companies when they originally collected their data and how often they update their lists.

You will probably also use your own mailing list developed from open houses, special events and parents who telephoned your center. To avoid wasting money on postage, keep your mailing list updated. Remove names of families who have moved out of your area.

IMPORTANT: Try your flyer out on a small number of homes. This lets you test the mailing list and the effectiveness of your flyer. If you can afford it, you may even want to try two or three different flyers to different households to see if one is more effective than another.

Most experts say to expect no more than one- to two-percent response to a direct mail piece. If that is cost-effective for you, and you get a good response from your mailing, consider doing another, larger mailing.

Do your direct mail at times of the year when parents are looking for child care. The end of summer, late December or early January and late spring (for summer programs) are the best times.

TIP

Some of your direct mail costs can be held down by getting bulk rates on postage. Check with your post office or direct mail company if you are buying a mailing list.

In Chapter 1, I discussed how to design a flyer (see Idea #10). I have listed some ways to distribute flyers below. This is only a beginning. You are limited only by your imagination and the number of flyers you or your staff can circulate in your community.

Where do your prospective parents gather? These are the places to leave flyers about your program.

Try:

- Pediatricians' offices
- Doctors' offices
- Local schools
- Children's clothing stores
- Laundromats
- Model homes
- Real estate agents
- Welcome Wagon
- Children's fairs
- Banks
- Libraries
- Shoe stores
- Grocery stores

Check to see if your community has an anti-litter ordinance. If so, you may need to pay for the cleanup of your flyers that people toss on the ground.

A nice way to display your flyers is placing them in "Take One" or "point of sale" racks. These are plastic holders that allow you to attractively show off your program. Business owners in your neighborhood are often glad to let you distribute your flyers in their shops or offices if you professionally display them in this type of rack. Take the racks to places your prospective parents gather. Libraries, pediatricians' offices, dentists' offices and children's clothing shops are good places. Add the word "free" to the outside of the rack and more people will pick one up.

Some local shops and offices won't let you display flyers that advertise your program. If this happens to you, use "Take One" racks to distribute educational flyers about child care or parenting. There are a number of sources for this type of pamphlet, including NAEYC (see Idea #16). Put your "Compliments of . . . " sticker on each pamphlet and also on the rack itself. Since the pamphlets are not directly advertising your center, office managers and owners usually will allow you to leave a rack on their counter. You benefit by becoming known as a resource for information about young children, which eventually leads to enrollments in your program.

PUBLICITY

When you use publicity, you use the media to raise public awareness about your center and the services you offer. You also receive recognition and support for the activities of your parents, children and staff.

The good news about publicity is that it's free. You do not pay a nickel for your name to appear in the media. Publicity is also very believable. It is referred to as "third party endorsement." A third party – in this case, the media – is telling the public about your good deeds. People find this type of information much more believable than if you told them yourself. Third party endorsements give you credibility in the community. They enhance your image in the community and create good will.

The bad news about publicity is that you have no control over what the media says about you. You also have no control over when and where an article or story appears. If it does appear, it may not be flattering and it may not be accurate. Working with the media also takes time. It takes time to write press releases and time to develop contacts in the media.

If you think the time and effort is worth it, read on. Here are a few tips to help you work with the media and to make the most of the coverage you receive.

What is your hook? Is your story newsworthy? This is called developing a "hook." What types of stories "hook" reporters and readers? Lucky for us, they love stories about children. Imagine how difficult it would be to develop a newsworthy story if you managed a laundromat. In this section, I've listed several activities that lend themselves well to media coverage. Use them along with activities in the "Community Marketing" section of this book and any other special activities in your center that would make a good story.

Press releases. A press release is the primary way to get an editor's attention. There are very specific guidelines to writing a press release. They are simple to learn and are described in detail in a number of publications. I strongly recommend the Child Care Action Campaign's Media Kit, which you can get by calling (212) 239-0138. Another excellent resource is the *Media Resource Guide*, published by the Foundation for American Communications (FACS). It is available for $10 from FACS, 3800 Barham Blvd, Suite 409, Los Angeles, CA 90068 or by calling (213) 851-7372.

You need to send your press release to the right person. Send it to a specific department and to the appropriate editor. If you don't know, call the newspaper, radio or TV station for names. George Doe will probably pay more attention to a release sent directly to him than to one sent To Whom It May Concern. Send "hard" news to the city, news or business editor. Send holiday or "soft" news to the feature editor.

It works best if you can hand the release directly to the right editor. It's even better if you know him or her. Check with your parents to see if any of them work for or know someone in the media who can help you. There's a good chance someone knows someone in the media. If you join a community civic group or Chamber of Commerce, you will probably meet someone who is either from the media, or more likely, someone who knows someone. Use your contacts.

Enclose a black and white glossy photograph with every release. Your chance of getting published increase 1000 percent with a photo.

What do you do if no one calls you? Try a follow-up telephone call. If you don't have time to call, simply keep sending out those press releases. It is not uncommon for a director to send out ten press releases with no response. Then a reporter calls on the eleventh!

Watch the papers even if you don't receive a telephone call. Neighborhood or local newspapers often run a picture with a caption or write a short story without ever calling you. This is especially true if you send a photograph.

What do you do when a story appears in the paper? Make reprints of every article that appears. Give one to each of your parents. When you mail a brochure to a prospective parent, include the reprint. Put one in each enrollment packet. If it appeared in a magazine, frame it and put it on the wall in your reception area. Use your imagination to get as much mileage as possible from this powerful "third party" endorsement.

If you land a television appearance, tell your parents. Most will be delighted to see their early childhood program featured on television. Do not assume the story will appear that day. If you ask, most reporters will call you to tell you when the story will air. This is also true for newspaper reporters.

TIP

Get signed releases from all parents before you take a picture of a child for the press or have a television crew tape them. Include a blanket release form with enrollment papers and keep them on file. A release form protects you from parents coming back later and suing you for publicizing their child without their permission.

The ideas in this section are all ways that you and the children in your center can help make your community a better place to live. If you also promote these activities in the media, you have the added benefit of increased exposure to new families who value community involvement. Your present families will be proud to have their children in a program that takes an active role in the community, even if the story never appears in the media.

While it is not repeated in each activity in this section, remember to contact the media by sending a press release and black and white glossy photo, followed by a telephone call. Over time, your perseverance will pay off.

Here are a few ideas that have been successful media attention-getters for other directors.

IDEA 51 HOLIDAY GIVING

Take a Christmas tree to a shelter for homeless families, a shelter for domestic violence victims, a center for abused and neglected children or a group home for children. Have your children decorate it with ornaments they made themselves. Bring a snack of muffins and juice to share with all the children.

IDEA 52 EMERGENCY ASSISTANCE

If there is a crisis or emergency in your area, such as an earthquake, fire or flood, have all your families and children pitch in to help. Collect clothing, have a bake sale to collect money, have a food drive and call the media. Ask a TV station if they would like to film the children working on the project in your center, then follow the children as they give the money or goods to the Red Cross or other organization.

IDEA 53 CLOTHING DRIVE

During August, collect children's clothing for families who cannot afford to buy back-to-school outfits for their children. Ask your families to donate children's clothing. Put up notices in local neighborhood businesses, asking other families to donate as well. When your center is a clothing collection point, you also receive many new visitors to your program. Send the clothing to the Salvation Army or other charitable agency for distribution.

IDEA 54 TREE PLANTING

Plant a tree on the grounds of a new elementary school in your neighborhood or in a local park. Erect a permanent plaque near the tree with the name of your center and the date you planted the tree. Don't forget your logo and street address.

IDEA 55 ***CELEBRATE YOUR BUSINESS ANNIVERSARY***

Celebrate your business anniversary with a neighborhood party, fair or special donation to a children's program. This is newsworthy if you are in a small town. If you are located in a larger city, try your local community newspapers.

IDEA 56 ***WORKING WITH SENIOR ADULTS***

There are many opportunities for your children to interact with senior adults in your community. Many of you already have ongoing relationships with nursing homes and adult day care centers. If not, consider contacting a senior adult center to ask if they would like your children to visit.

There are many ways the children in your program can interact with senior adults. The adults can visit your center or you can visit them. You can play games together, sing together and have parties together. Try hosting Thanksgiving dinner, showing off your Halloween costumes or having a regularly scheduled story time. Always remember to maintain the dignity of older adults when planning activities that are also developmentally appropriate for your children.

Purchase or develop a pamphlet about how to choose quality child care. Most local resource and referral agencies have this type of pamphlet, as does NAEYC. During peak enrollment times, like August, let the media know that you will send free copies of this brochure to those who write or call for it. This helps to establish you as an expert and a resource on child care in your community. If you can afford it, don't ask for a self-addressed, stamped envelope. You want to put the pamphlet in your own envelope with your logo on it. Put your "Compliments of . . . " sticker on each pamphlet (see Idea #17). This pamphlet is "no strings attached." Don't send your own brochure with it, but you can put their names on your mailing list for future events.

REFERRALS

Before you read this section, ask ten people you know to describe your center. Do they know enough about you to recommend your program? If not, how can you provide them with additional information?

Personal recommendations or referrals are the most cost-effective way to build enrollment in early childhood programs. In our field, parents use personal recommendations as the preferred way to choose a program. However, most of us just wait for referrals. We don't do much to encourage them. Is there a way to encourage referrals? Absolutely. Reach out to potential referral sources to be sure they have information about your program. Then ask them for referrals.

Most successful centers do not rely solely on referrals. While they are a powerful source for child care programs, referrals alone will not build your enrollment. Use referrals along with other marketing tools to build enrollment. After your center is full, you can cut back on some of your marketing efforts. You can use word-of-mouth referrals to fill your occasional openings.

When should you not promote personal referrals?

Do not promote personal referrals if your program is no better than average. You will be wasting your time. People will refer families to you only if they are highly satisfied and comfortable with your program.

Here's an example. Suppose the Olson family is enrolled in your program. Mrs. Olson's neighbor and good friend, Ms. Brown, needs a program for her child and Mrs. Olson recommends your center. Now suppose Ms. Brown calls your center. The person who answers the phone knows little about the program or doesn't know where you are. She asks Ms. Brown to call back later. Or perhaps the phone call goes well, but when Ms. Brown comes to visit she sees a chaotic office, a director who is harried or a classroom that is out of control. Ms. Brown is obviously not going to enroll her child. More importantly, she will probably relate her experience to Mrs. Olson. Mrs. Olson will undoubtedly be embarrassed and will make excuses ("I'm sure you caught them on a bad day"). Mrs. Olson will vow never to recommend you again.

As you can see, referrals are very personal and something to cherish. The following section offers you ways to encourage positive referrals.

Ford Motor Company estimates that a *satisfied* car owner tells *eight* people that he or she is pleased, while a *dissatisfied* one tells *twenty-two* people. Keep your families satisfied. Happy parents refer others to your center. The best way to encourage referrals is to offer a high quality program and resolve parent problems and complaints as quickly as possible.

IDEA **58** *STAFF REFERRALS*

Have you thought about your staff as referral sources? A satisfied and knowledgeable staff member can be one of your best sources for new families.

Staff members need to know all about the program. Staff should know how to talk about your program in terms of benefits, instead of features (see Idea #75). They should know which rooms have openings currently and which ones will have openings soon. They should be familiar with other programs in the area and know what makes your program best. They generally should not talk about tuition rates, since rates vary among age groups and depend on the number of days or hours a child attends. They can say, "I don't know exactly what the tuition is, but I know it is competitive with other programs in our area," or "It is less than other programs in our area." Give them the words to use. You may want to use your monthly staff meetings to keep employees informed about these issues.

Most of all, your employees should be happy working in your center. They should enjoy coming to work, feel fulfilled in their jobs and truly believe in your program. Unhappy employees are like unhappy customers. They project a negative image and will turn parents away.

IDEA 59   REFERRALS FROM YOUR VAN DRIVER

I have listed your van driver as a separate referral source. This person is an important and highly visible goodwill ambassador for your program. Make sure the driver is dressed appropriately, drives well and smiles. Give the driver an engraved name badge (see Idea #9). The driver should have an ample supply of business cards and brochures in the van to give to interested parents.

IDEA 60   PEOPLE YOU INTERVIEW FOR JOBS

Every time you interview a prospective employee, you and your center are also being interviewed. Even if you do not hire a person, you leave an impression, positive or negative. Most potential employees come from your neighborhood, which is also the source of most of your prospective families.

What can you do to foster referrals from people you interview? Make sure each one leaves with your business card and a brochure about your program. If you have time, give the interviewee a tour of your center. Describe each room and any special services you provide to families. If you use this technique, you will be amazed at the number of referrals that come to you from your interviewees.

IDEA 61 · REFERRALS FROM YOUR FRIENDS AND NEIGHBORS

Who knows you and your reputation better than your friends? While you will undoubtedly feel uncomfortable "selling" your program to friends and neighbors, you can let them know about your program in general conversation. Talk about ages you serve, program hours, fees, where you have openings, special promotions and special features, such as a pool, a great outdoor area, computers and highly qualified staff. Leave your business card and a brochure with them. When parents ask your friends and neighbors about early childhood programs in the area, they will have enough information to refer those families to you.

IDEA 62 · MUTUAL REFERRALS

Become familiar with other early childhood programs in your area. Establish a system of mutual referrals if their goals and program quality are consistent with yours. If your two-year-old room is full and theirs is not, refer the family to the other program. They will do the same for you. Everyone benefits from this approach. Families appreciate your thoughtfulness and will often refer other families to you, even though they could not enroll themselves. You also benefit from referrals from the other programs. Make sure you keep in regular touch with these programs to let them know your needs and to monitor their quality.

Look for other professionals who have offices near your center. Good sources are children's clothing shops, dentists, pediatricians, children's furniture stores, family-oriented restaurants, shoe stores and real estate agents. You can have a mutual referral system with those who offer compatible products or services. Agree to distribute each other's flyers or brochures. Do this only with professionals and business owners you know and trust. You don't want to refer someone to a pediatrician who has a rude office staff or who consistently leaves patients in the waiting room for hours.

IDEA  **REAL ESTATE AGENTS**

Real estate agents can be good referral sources for your program. Every time new families buy homes in your neighborhood, real estate agents can tell them about your center. You can send flyers to the agents, but most agents like to refer new parents if they have had personal contact with you. Take time to meet them.

What's the best approach? Most agents recommend that you host a luncheon. Send out invitations and ask for an RSVP. If you tell them there will be a drawing for a $50 gift certificate at a local department store, your response will be even higher. Make sure each agent leaves the luncheon with a business card and brochures about your program.

Time after time directors have told me stories about suppliers referring families to their program. Who are your suppliers? The companies and individuals who provide your food, educational toys and furniture, maintenance, lawn service and repairs are all potential referral sources. Once I actually received a referral from our plumber who was so impressed with our small toilets, he told his neighbor about them.

How do you encourage referrals from your suppliers? First and foremost, be friendly when they visit. Show them your school. Pay your bills on time. Always include your business card when you pay your bill.

Some service-oriented businesses feel so strongly about supplier referrals that they send each supplier an annual satisfaction questionnaire, asking questions like these:

- Are we accessible?
- Are we reliable with our payments?
- Are we polite when you come to our center?
- Do you have any comments to share with us?

IDEA **RESOURCE AND REFERRAL AGENCIES**

Many communities today have resource and referral (R & R) agencies that help parents find child care. Get to know the people who work directly with parents. Invite them to your center for lunch. Send them your newsletter. Send handwritten notes about any new programs you are offering. Call them once in a while to say hello. Frequent contact with R & R agencies will make you more than a listing in the R & R computer.

IDEA **ASK FOR REFERRALS**

Ask your parents for referrals. This sounds overly simple, but most of us do not do it. You can do this in a tasteful manner without looking desperate. Let parents know when you have openings, especially in other rooms. They may think that because their two-year-old child's room is full, all the others are as well.

To stimulate word-of-mouth referrals, give your current parents several copies of a flyer that announces a new service at your school. You can also give them copies of your brochure in August and January, when other parents often change their existing child care arrangements. Attach a note to the flyers or brochures, letting them know that you are making the brochures or flyers available for them to share with friends if they wish.

IDEA **SHORT BROCHURE**

Consider developing a short brochure solely for new families. Families are most likely to talk with others about your program within their first thirty days of enrollment. This brochure thanks them for their enrollment and lists your program's special benefits and features. This gesture gives new families a good feeling about you, as well as information to pass on to others.

If you try this idea, give the brochure to your new parents on their first day. Do not give it to them with other paperwork or it will lose its impact.

IDEA **THANK YOU FOR REFERRALS**

It is absolutely essential to say "thank you" to each and every person who refers a new family to your program. Don't forget your staff who make referrals. Send a personal note to each one.

Some programs offer a tuition credit if parents refer a new family. Other centers give savings bonds to families who refer.

Consider sending flowers or a small gift to the referring parent's work place. The cost of a gift is a small percentage of the first week's tuition. The tuition will continue for many months or years. Your thoughtful gesture will multiply the number of referrals you get. Choose a gift that can be placed on a desk and include a note thanking the parent for the referral. An added benefit is that the parent will probably share the gift with fellow employees, who also may be prospective parents.

THE ENROLLMENT PROCESS

You've begun promoting your program in the community, and now you're waiting for parents to call and enroll in your program. Wait! Just because they call, doesn't mean they're ready to enroll. It's important to remember that your goal when a parent calls is to schedule an enrollment visit. And your goal when a parent visits is to enroll the child. This sounds simple, but many directors spend too much time talking about the program on the telephone and forget to ask the parent to visit.

Track who calls, how they heard about you and how many people who call also come in to visit. This is your "call-to-visit" ratio. How many who visit and also enroll their children is your "visit-to-enroll" ratio. If you're getting lots of telephone calls, but not many visits, you need to work on your telephone skills. If parents come to visit, but do not enroll, you need to examine the enrollment visit.

I don't take a sales approach in this chapter. I prefer to think about it as "public relations." There are books and tapes that can help you learn how to "close the sale" with parents. I'm not focusing on that approach in this book, however, because I think many directors are uncomfortable when they feel they are "selling" their schools. If this describes you, that's okay. You may not enroll as many families as the director who likes to "sell," but if you fake it, parents will see your discomfort. Just be yourself and incorporate the ideas in this chapter. If you do want to learn more about how to become comfortable with a soft selling approach to building enrollment, I recommend Julie Wasson's audio cassette learning program called, "Basic Techniques for Securing Enrollment." It is loaded with great ideas for incorporating a soft selling approach to building enrollment in your center. You can order her cassette tapes by calling The Julian Group at 1-800-876-0260.

TELEPHONE TIPS

"I screened many centers over the phone. I would never take my child there the way they talked to me."

I heard this comment in a focus group of parents and saw all the other parents in the group nod in agreement. Hopefully, that parent was not talking about your program or mine!

But I still wonder how many people called my center and didn't come to visit because of the way the telephone was answered. The first impression someone has of your center is often from a phone call. Ask yourself these questions to see if your program is losing potential families over the phone.

Where do you answer the phone? If a parent can hear children in the background, it sounds chaotic, even if it really isn't.

Who answers the telephone? At 7:00 a.m.? At 5:30 p.m.? That's often when working parents make their telephone calls.

How long does it take for someone to answer the phone? Imagine what goes through a parent's mind when no one answers the telephone. Your phone should always be answered no later than during the third ring.

Finally, remember your goal when a parent calls. It is not to convince the parent to enroll. It is to schedule a visit to your program. Use the ideas in this section to improve your telephone skills and increase the number of visits to your program.

Keep detailed records of people who telephone you. I have included a sample form in the appendix that you may want to use. Some directors use 8 1/2 x 11 paper, while others prefer having the forms printed on large note cards. Keep blank forms near all your telephones. Get each caller's name and address whenever possible to send a brochure. Ask how the person found your center. Was it from the Yellow Pages, a referral from a friend or an ad? You'll find this information helpful as you plan your future marketing expenditures.

Make notes about the names and ages of the children, along with any concerns or needs the parent expresses. You can reference these in your follow-up note ("I know this will be Maria's first time in a preschool program. At ABC Preschool, we have many children just like Maria and work hard to make this first experience a positive one for her."). The notes will also help you when the parent calls again or comes for a visit. Review the notes before the visit to directly address the parents' needs during the visit. Finding a new program is a difficult, emotional process for parents. Remembering the child's name and the parents' specific needs go a long way to show parents that you offer a caring program that stands out from your competition.

IDEA  *SMILE*

Smile when you answer the telephone. People can hear you smile over the phone. Smiling changes the tone in your voice. No matter how frazzled you feel or how stressed you are, take a deep breath and smile as you answer your telephone. It works! Smiling is the least expensive but most powerful marketing tool in your arsenal.

IDEA  *ANSWERING THE TELEPHONE*

Answer your telephone the same way each time. Always use the center's name, your name and a greeting. Try, "Good morning. Thank you for calling ABC Preschool. This is Diane. May I help you?" or "ABC Preschool. This is Diane, the director. How may I help you?" When parents call a number of programs, they often forget who said what. Mentioning your center's name will help the parent remember it.

We all dislike being placed on hold when we call a business. As a matter of fact, many callers hang up rather than sit on hold. Don't put someone on hold without their permission. Offer to call the person back.

If you or a staff member must put someone on hold, tell the caller the name of the person with whom they will be speaking. The staff member could say, "Our director, Ann Pace, is in one of the classrooms. I've paged Ann and she will be right with you." You will find the caller will wait longer when they have a name.

Think about having music on hold. People prefer this to silence. In addition, there is a company in California called "Information on Hold" that can tape a special message about your center to play while callers are on hold.

At some time or another we all have inadvertently left parents on hold for long periods of time. Consider having telephones that ring back automatically to remind you that you placed a person on hold.

ASK QUESTIONS AND LISTEN TO RESPONSES

Nothing is more frustrating to me than a sales clerk who tries to sell me something without first asking what I need. It happened recently when I went to buy a new answering machine for my office. I walked into the store and told the salesperson that I needed an answering machine. He walked right over to the machines and said, "Here they are. I really like this one. It is easy to use and you can pick up your calls from anywhere . . . ." All this before even asking me what I needed. He should have asked if the answering machine was for my home or office. How many telephone lines did I have? Did I already have an answering machine? Why was I looking for a new one? And so on.

When parents call your center, remember how you felt when a salesperson didn't bother to ask what you needed. Find out why the parent is looking for a program. Is it the child's first time in an early childhood center? Ask them about their child's last child care program. What is most important to them in a program? Have they had any problems in other programs that they would like to avoid?

The answers to these questions will provide a wealth of information about the parent's child care needs. Their answers will help you talk about your program in terms that are important to the parent. Write down the questions and keep them on a card near your telephone. When you are busy, it's difficult to remember all the questions you need to ask.

And most importantly, listen to what parents have to say. Concentrate. Don't think about what you are going to say next while the parent is still talking. Avoid interrupting the parent. This seems like simplistic advice, but you'll be surprised how much additional information parents give when they sense you are a good listener.

Talk about your program in terms of its benefits to parents, rather than its features. This is one of the hardest things to learn, but it is very effective when you work with parents. What's the difference between benefits and features? When you are talking about your program's features, you are discussing the facts. Features are your hours, services you offer, your location and your extracurricular programs. When you discuss benefits, you look at your program from the parents' perspective. You're talking about what they receive, rather than what you have.

Let's look at an example. If you were describing your center's features, you'd say, "Our hours are 6:30 a.m.-6:30 p.m., Monday through Friday." If you were discussing your program's benefits, you'd say, "We know how hard it is for you to find a child care program with flexible hours. Your schedule as a working parent is very challenging. I understand how hard it is for you to leave work at 5:00 and race through rush hour traffic to pick up your child. That's why we stay open from 6:30 a.m. to 6:30 p.m. You will have plenty of time to get home from work to pick up your child." Can you see the difference now? Your center's feature is your hours. The benefit to parents is convenience and flexibility.

This technique works best when you already have some information from the parent (see Ideas #70 and #74). Suppose a mother told you that an educational program is very important to her. The parent also said that Sandy is an only child and hasn't played much with other children. You can use this information later in the conversation when you say, "I know how important it is to you for Sandy to have a good educational experience. Here at ABC Preschool, Sandy will receive plenty of individualized attention as she learns at her own pace. Sandy will have lots of experience working, sharing and playing with other children to develop her social skills, which you also said was important to you, Ms. Martin." In these examples, you are focusing on the benefits to families, not your program's features.

Compare that to what you might normally say. "Here at ABC Preschool, we provide an individualized program that allows children to learn at their own pace. We also work on other areas of development, such as social skills." Which approach sounds better to you?

I have included a features and benefits worksheet in the appendix. Practice with the worksheet, then start using your program's benefits when you talk to parents. You'll be amazed at how much more responsive they will be.

Personalize the call from a prospective parent by using the parent's name during the telephone conversation. It is flattering to a caller when you remember his or her name and the child's name as well.

Avoid using the caller's first name. Some people may feel it is impolite to use their first name before they tell you to. Even if they are not offended, using a person's title and last name shows respect, a feeling you want to convey to parents. Use Mr., Mrs. or Ms. and the caller's last name as you speak on the phone.

Too often we forget the main purpose for a telephone inquiry. It's to arrange a visit for the prospective parent. We are so busy taking down an address and telephone number, or giving out tuition information, that we forget to ask, "Would you like to make an appointment to visit our center?" You can even be more direct. "I really would like to show you our preschool. Can we make arrangements for a visit next Wednesday, or would Thursday be better for you?" or "I know Marissa would love our three-year-old class. Is it convenient to visit us in the morning, or would you prefer to come after work?" As you can see, these phrases don't ask, "Do you want to make an appointment?" The answer might be "no." The phrases I suggest assume the parent is coming and give them a choice of days or times. Parents must go out of the way to say they don't want to visit. It is a direct approach and it works. If you are uncomfortable being this direct (I am), try writing down these phrases and keep them by the telephone. It helps.

IDEA  **ENDING THE CALL**

When you close a conversation with a prospective parent, mention the name of your center again. Parents call several centers and often forget which one they just called, especially if they use the Yellow Pages. Say the caller's name again and say thank you for calling. Try, "Thank you for calling ABC Preschool, Ms. Ramirez. Goodbye," or "Thank you for calling ABC Preschool, Ms. Ramirez. I'll put a brochure in the mail to you this afternoon."

IDEA  **FOLLOW-UP**

Send a brochure and a follow-up note to every parent who calls you. Personalize the note with information you collected during the telephone call (see Idea #74). Put each name on your mailing list. The most important names on your mailing list are the people who call you for information. Send them newsletters, invitations to open houses and notices about special events. For more information about your mailing list, see Idea #11.

IDEA **80** *AN UNANSWERED TELEPHONE*

Never let your telephone go unanswered. Nothing strikes fear into the heart of a current parent more than the first time they call the center and no one answers the phone. Has the center burned down? Is there a problem? How's my baby?? I have known parents who changed child care programs because the telephone was chronically not answered. What if there was a family emergency and a parent really needed to talk to you?

If you don't have a telephone in one of your classrooms, don't have an assistant or there is some other reason you can't always cover your telephones, invest in an answering machine. Use it sparingly, however, since many people will hang up when they hear one, especially prospective parents. See Idea #81 for ideas to make an answering machine work for you.

An answering machine can be useful for the rare occasion when no one is available to answer the telephone. Use it sparingly. Two out of three people who reach an answering machine don't leave a message. Those numbers may be changing because of the proliferation of answering machines and voice mail. But when prospective parents reach an answering machine, they might just hang up and call the next program on the list.

If you decide to use an answering machine, the following tips will increase the machine's effectiveness as a marketing tool:

- Tell the caller where you are and why you aren't in your office. Say, "Hello, you have reached ABC Preschool. This is Joanie, the director. I'm in one of the classrooms right now and am not available to answer your call . . . ."

- Whenever possible, include in your message an alternative telephone number for the caller to use in an emergency.

- Check your answering machine every fifteen to twenty minutes. Set an egg timer or the alarm on your watch to remind yourself. On your answering machine message, tell the caller that you check the machine every half hour and will return the call at that time. Then do so. You give parents a very clear message about your reliability when you return calls when you say you will.

- If you have an answering machine that interrupts people after one minute of talking, get rid of it. Buy one that allows people to talk as long as they want.

82

I recently read about a national sales company that receives all of its sales leads from telephone calls. The company increased its "lead conversion rate," the number of inquiry calls converted to actual sales, 22 *percent* by teaching telephone manners and techniques. All your staff members should know how you want the telephone answered. It is unrealistic to expect them to know how you want the phone answered unless you teach them.

Plan telephone training sessions for your staff. You can bring someone in to conduct them or you can do it yourself. Talk about how to and how not to answer the telephone, what to say, what to do if an administrator is not available to talk with a parent and how to convey a friendly attitude on the telephone. Many directors believe it is best to have only certain people talk to parents about the program and the rates. If you agree, teach the rest of your staff how to effectively take a message.

It is best to repeat this type of training every few months. Answering the telephone is not the most important part of your teachers' jobs. They may forget key points without periodic refresher training.

Have a more specialized training session for staff members who are designated to give parents detailed information over the telephone. This training includes how to gather information, how to describe the program in terms of benefits to parents, how to ask parents questions about their child care needs and, most importantly, how to convert the telephone call into an enrollment visit.

IDEA **83** *CONVERTING YOUR CALLS INTO VISITS*

Your goal is to translate calls into visits to your center. Track how many of your telephone inquiries from parents turn into visits. If the percentage is low, you need to take a look at your telephone style. Why are parents not coming to visit after calling? Is the person answering the telephone knowledgeable about your program? Is there distracting background noise that makes your program sound disorganized? Are you talking about the benefits of your program, or just giving tuition information? Are you asking callers to visit?

These are the questions to ask yourself. You might have someone be a "mystery shopper" for your center. See Idea #84 to see how mystery shoppers work.

IDEA **84** **MYSTERY SHOPPER**

Mystery shoppers are commonly used in retail stores. They are hired by management to pretend to be customers. The shoppers report back how well they were treated by the store's sales clerks.

Ask a friend or colleague to be a telephone mystery shopper for you. Ask the person to call your center at different times during the day and pretend to be a parent looking for an early childhood program. Give the person a checklist of items to look for. Was the person who answered the phone courteous? Did she ask for the parent's name and describe the program in terms of benefits instead of features? Tell your staff that you are doing this and that the mystery shopper will not only be calling them, but you too. When you get positive feedback from the mystery shopper, let your staff know. Retail stores often give awards to sales clerks who receive good reports. When you get negative feedback, use the results for training sessions.

THE ENROLLMENT VISIT

You've talked on the telephone and scheduled a visit. Here comes the easy part, right? Right, as long as you're prepared. If you are already doing everything in this next section, enrolling new children should be a snap.

The purpose of the enrollment visit is to enroll the family. Don't forget to ask. We often show our center off, give great tours, and then don't say to the parent, "When would you like your daughter Maria to start?" Don't forget to ask this key question. It shows your interest in the family. It is another way of saying that you want to help this parent care for his or her child.

First impressions are lasting. This means the appearance of your center and staff, especially the director, are extremely important.

Parents who visit you have very little information about you prior to their visit. They will judge you by appearances first. Suppose you have an excellent program, but your office and reception area are cluttered. Most likely they see your office and reception area first and their first impression is that you are messy. Unconsciously they conclude that your program must also be disorganized. It is very difficult to overcome that first impression.

It is difficult for us to see how parents view our center. We practically live there and we are too close to be objective. We don't see the weeds in the parking lot, the cigarette butts on the sidewalk or the worn spot on the carpet. Walk through your parking lot, building and playground, looking through the eyes of a brand-new parent. Better yet, ask a trusted and honest friend to walk with you. Do not take your tour at 10:00 a.m. Walk around at 7:30 a.m., right before lunch and 5:30 p.m.

Look around your parking lot.

- Is it free of weeds and trash?

- Is the exterior of your building well maintained?

- Are there terse, handwritten notes on the front door reminding parents to pay their tuition or is the door attractive and inviting?

In your lobby area, use your senses.

- What do you see? Is your reception area parent- and child-oriented? Is there an adult present to greet you? If there are children in the lobby, are they well-behaved and supervised by an adult?

- What do you hear? Chaos? Nothing? Or pleasant sounds of children playing and working?

- What do you smell? Disinfectant? Urine? Or the smell of coffee, spices or cookies from the kitchen?

There are many excellent checklists to help you with program quality. Harms and Clifford's *Early Childhood Environment Rating Scales* are excellent. If you do not already use an evaluation form for your program, I suggest you start now. The following questions about the appearance of your classrooms and playground refer to what parents see during a tour.

When you walk into a classroom, what do you see?

- Is the room child-oriented? Is it cheerful? Is children's art mounted on the walls at their level?

- Does the teacher acknowledge visitors with a smile and a friendly greeting?

- Are the adults in the room acting as traffic cops? Or are they interacting positively with children?

- What is happening in the room? Are children running around? Or are they happily involved in projects and activities?

- Is the room chaotically noisy? Too quiet? Or humming with the sounds of busy children?

- Is it obvious that there are planned activities occurring in the room?

- If you offer infant and toddler care, how do these rooms smell? Are all of the awake infants out of their cribs? Are all toddlers happily involved with activities?

David Gleason wrote an excellent article entitled, "Impressions: How One Parent Reacts When Visiting Centers," that appeared in the May 1987 issue of *Child Care Information Exchange*. In the article, he asks a key question about your outdoor area: "Would I have fun on this playground?"

- Is there lots to do outdoors? Are there enough trikes, wagons, balls and shovels?

- Is there plenty of shade for hot summer days?

- Are there inviting patches of grass for children to sit on, roll down or run through?

- Is the equipment in good condition? Have the splinters and cobwebs on the climbing structures been removed? Have all the broken buckets and rusted trucks been thrown away?

- Are the teachers talking among themselves? Or are they interacting with the children?

This list is by no means an exhaustive one. Use it as a starting point. Make your own checklist. Walk through your center. Note what you like and what needs changing. You probably will not be able to change everything at once, but develop a schedule and make the changes as soon as you can.

While we are on the touchy subject of appearances, it is important to discuss the dress and demeanor of staff members. Dress codes are very difficult for most staff members. In each center I directed, we had a dress code that was developed by the staff. I always talked to them about parents' first impressions (see Idea #85). I know what teachers wear has nothing to do with their ability to teach, but I also know parents usually do not know how to evaluate early childhood programs. Most of them, when they don't have much information, look at the teachers' appearance and make judgments based on that. I must admit, even as a professional, I have a hard time overcoming my first impressions of a teacher in a dirty sweatshirt and sweat pants, or in shorts so short that little is left to the imagination. Having simple dress guidelines that everyone helps develop, along with the requirement that all staff members be neat and well-groomed, go a long way to creating positive first impressions.

The director's appearance is perhaps even more important than the staff's, since parents usually meet the director first. Numerous focus groups with parents have shown that parents are most comfortable when the director of their early childhood program looks professional. This doesn't mean suits or high heels. It does mean a nice skirt or pair of slacks. I like full skirts so I can also sit comfortably on the floor with children. Dress is only one component of a director's appearance, though. Are you calm and in control? Are you ready for the parent's visit or did you forget about it until the parent walked in the door? Do you have enrollment papers ready and have you reviewed the parent's personal information taken on the telephone? Are you smiling? If the answer to all these questions is "yes," you're on your way.

IDEA **87** *SMILE*

Think about it. When was the last time you visited a business and the owner or manager smiled at you? It doesn't happen automatically, does it? Your smile is one of your least expensive but most compelling marketing tools. Greeting a prospective parent with a genuine and sincere smile goes a long way toward putting parents at ease and making them feel at home.

Your smile tells prospective parents many things about you. It says that you are warm, approachable, likable and enjoy your work. Your smile begins the bonding process that is so important between you and the families you serve. Yet a director's day can become so hectic that it's easy to forget to smile. If you need to, write the word "SMILE" on your parent inquiry card to remind you of your smile's importance when parents visit your program.

THE "HOW TO CHOOSE CHILD CARE" PAMPHLET

Give parents a "how to choose" pamphlet during the enrollment tour and use it to promote your program's benefits. Talk about key points during your tour, describing how you meet or exceed the standards on the checklist. Also, talk freely about what parents should look for in centers. Most parents don't know what to look for. We provide an important service by giving them this information. Parents appreciate these tips. If you truly feel that your program excels, you are qualified to tell parents what to look for in a quality program.

During the tour, focus on the competitive advantages of your center. For example, suppose your staff/child ratios are the best in the neighborhood. As you're walking in the two-year-old room, say:

"The number of staff members in each room is very important in an early childhood program. The state requires that we have one staff person for every eight two-year-olds, but here at ABC Preschool, we believe two-year-olds need lots of adult attention. Our ratios here are one adult to every six children. If you visit other centers, you should ask what their ratios are. Visit the room and count the number of staff and children yourself."

In this example, you are doing a number of things:

- You are helping parents learn what to look for, such as staff/child ratios.

- You are providing the information at their level. You told them why staff/child ratios are important ("two-year-olds need lots of adult attention").

- You are featuring one of your competitive advantages, that is, your excellent staff/child ratios.

Parents like this approach for two reasons:

- They find that you offer something special for their child.

- They learn something new about how to find a quality program.

You can use this technique for anything you offer that your competition does not. It could be a special playground, a developmentally appropriate curriculum or superior staff qualifications. Do your homework. Know your competition and be current about the changes they make in their programs. You do not want to brag about your playground, telling parents about how important a park-like environment is, only to find out later that the XYZ Preschool down the street has just put in a new playground that looks just as good if not better than yours.

Have a program policy that promotes positive separation between parent and child. Write down your policy and share it with all prospective families during your enrollment tour. For example, you may wish to invite a parent to stay on the child's first morning. Work together as a group with your staff to decide how you can best foster a positive separation experience for new families, then implement it in each room. Parents will certainly be impressed with your concern and care for their child. Here are some ideas to get you started:

- Have a cubby for the new child already labeled with his or her name before the child arrives.

- Let the other children in the room know that there is going to be someone new.

- Encourage the child to bring a favorite cuddly toy from home to help ease separation from home and parents.

- Ask the parent for a picture of the family. Keep it easily accessible in the child's cubby, so the child can look at it as often as desired during those first few days in a strange environment.

- Talk with your staff about the anxieties that children face when they enter a new program and what each person can do to make it easier for children.

Also refer to additional ideas in the next chapter in the section titled "A Child's First Days."

Always follow up with a note after a parent has visited your program. Here are some tips to make your note more effective:

- Personalize the letter by mentioning the child's name. Also refer to something about the family's needs that you learned. For example, "I know how hard it is to find part-time care for Jonathan" or "Janie, our three-year-old teacher, is very good helping children make the move from family child care to a child care center. I know that's important to you for Ryan."

- Mention your program's competitive advantage, what makes it different from other programs, as it relates to the child. "Our small group sizes will really meet Johnny's needs as he makes the transition from your current family child care provider."

- Talk about how your program will meet their needs. Discuss benefits rather than features. "At ABC Preschool, we are very aware of working parents' schedules. That's why we open earlier than the other centers in our area."

- Write the note by hand and be sure it does not sound like a form letter.

IDEA 91 A SPECIAL BOOK

Write a simple book for children called, "My First Day at ABC Preschool." You can use photos or line drawings with a simple story about a typical day in your program. Give it to parents when they first enroll to read to their children before their first day at your center. It is a nice way to ease the transition into your program for young children. You might want to have more than one story, depending on how your schedule differs for toddlers and preschoolers.

ONCE THEY'RE ENROLLED

Communication, communication, communication. You will see this theme throughout this chapter.

$$1 = 27$$

Source: Marketing News, February 4, 1991.

What does "1 = 27" mean? For every one complaint that you receive, there are twenty-six additional parents who feel the same way, but did not speak up. These could be twenty-six unhappy parents who leave or twenty-six prospective parents who called but did not come in for a visit. It could be twenty-six parents who visited but did not enroll their children.

The issue is not that you cannot make mistakes. We all have bad days. The issue is how you handle the problem with parents afterwards.

Keep the lines of communication open. This chapter includes ideas for the "little things" that make new families feel welcome and your long-term families feel appreciated. While we all do some of these some of the time, it's easy to let the little things slip in the day-to-day hustle and bustle of our programs. This chapter includes ideas to help you keep those lines of communication open.

Jay Conrad Levinson, author of many marketing books, says that "smart business owners" spend 10 percent of their marketing budget on "talking to the universe in general," 30 percent on prospective customers and 60 percent on their satisfied customers. Why spend so much time and money on your current families? It is much less expensive to retain a family than recruit a new one. As a matter of fact, it generally costs a business five times as much to replace a customer as it does to retain one. Don't forget that *happy families refer other families*. Read on for some tried and true ideas.

A CHILD'S FIRST DAYS

There are many books and articles that talk about how to ease a child into a new early childhood program. For example, the August/September 1990 and August/September 1992 issues of *Pre-K Today* feature several excellent articles on parent/child separation.* The purpose of this section is not to discuss transitions from the child's point of view, but rather to look at it from the parent's perspective. Your aim is also to help parents feel good about choosing your program for their child.

Since the highest rate of withdrawal occurs within six to eight weeks of enrollment, the first few weeks a family is with you are the most important. Most of these ideas are common sense. See them as a jumping off point. Brainstorm with your staff about ways all of you can make new families feel welcome. Ask some of your parents what made them feel good about your program during those first weeks and what you could do to make it even better for other new families.

*For a few basic ideas for easing a new child's transition into your program, refer to Idea #89.

IDEA 92 WELCOME LETTER

Frequent and personal contact with new families is important. How many times have you "enrolled" a new child and the family fails to show up? In some programs it happens often. If it has happened to you, keep in contact with your families before they arrive. Shortly after the family enrolls, but before the child's first day, send a letter to the family welcoming them to your program. Include the pamphlet about separation from NAEYC, with your "Compliments of . . . " sticker attached, of course.

IDEA 93 HOME AND SCHOOL VISITS

If your resources allow it, arrange for your teacher to visit a new family's home before the child's first day in preschool. The child meets the teacher in familiar and comfortable surroundings. It also shows parents that you are concerned about their child.

IDEA **94** *BUDDY SYSTEM*

The first day in any new early childhood program is, at best, bewildering for a young child. To ease that transition, assign a buddy to the new child. The buddy is a child who has been in your program long enough to know the ropes and who is social enough to include the new child in activities. Learning about a new school from a buddy is often not as overwhelming to a new child as learning about it from an adult. Give the buddy a special name badge to wear for the next few days. Everyone "wins" with this system. The new child has an instant companion and the buddy learns responsibility and caring. Buddies should be at least three years old. Younger children do not yet understand how to be a buddy.

Send notes home to each set of parents, the buddy's and the new child's, to let them know about the buddy system. New parents will appreciate your caring and concern. Your buddy's parents will feel good that their child was chosen for such a special task.

 **WELCOME PHOTO**

Here's a good way to make new families feel they belong. New families are often apprehensive and it's important to help them feel at home. Take a Polaroid snapshot of each new family. Post it on your parent bulletin board, along with a note welcoming the new family to your program. You can do this on the family's first day, but sometimes first days are hectic or tearful. It might be better to take the picture earlier, perhaps when they give you a deposit or during the home visit.

IDEA  **TELLING PARENTS WHAT TO EXPECT**

Let parents of first-time child care enrollees know ahead of time that bumps, bruises and scratches are inevitable, as are colds and the flu. If a child has never been in group care, parents may overreact when the child comes home with an unexplained scrape or comes down with two colds in one season. If you let parents know ahead what to expect, the first bruise or cold won't be so upsetting. Make this a specific, but not overwhelming, part of your first on-site conversation with parents. Be careful. Too much emphasis will scare new parents. A good time to discuss accidents and illness is when observing a room with the parent and a child falls or cries and needs attention. You might also include a statement in your enrollment packet about this, as well as some comments on parent-child separation.

IDEA 97 SAYING GOODBYE

Don't let parents sneak out of the room without saying goodbye to their child. Some parents think it will make it easier for the child if they don't have tearful goodbyes. To build trust, though, children need to say goodbye and hear that the parents will return soon.

Schedule a time for parents to bring their child to your center before the child's first day. The visit can be short, between thirty minutes and one hour, ideally during a free choice activity time in the classroom. This visit gives the child a chance to spend time in the classroom with the parent present. The child has the opportunity to play with some of the toys and meet the other children. Younger children can spend time with the new teacher, while older children can meet the teacher and their buddy.

IDEA 98 CALLING PARENTS ON THE FIRST DAY

Call the parent during the child's first day to let him know how the day is going. Recount a positive activity of the child's day. For example, "Lana has a new friend. They've been playing in the block area this morning," or "Shauna made a beautiful collage for you in the art center today." Parents will feel relieved and grateful that you care enough to take the time to call.

IDEA 99   TAKE A PICTURE

On a child's first day in your program, take a Polaroid picture of the child involved in an indoor or outdoor activity. Put it in a cardboard frame that says, "My first day at ABC Preschool." Send it in the mail to the parent's work place, along with a letter thanking them for choosing your center. By sending pictures to the work place, parents most likely will put the pictures on their desks. This is an added exposure for your program.

IDEA 100   SENDING A NOTE AND PICTURE HOME

Ask each teacher to send a special note home sometime during the child's first week, describing in detail at least one activity in which the child was involved. If possible, include a Polaroid snapshot of the child engaged in an activity, preferably with another child or children. Label the picture with your center's name, date, name of the children in the photo and a nice caption for the picture. Refer to Idea #99 for another way to use a snapshot of a child's first day.

KEEPING CURRENT FAMILIES HAPPY

Did you know that 68 percent of people do not return to a business because of the attitude of the person who served them? Only 9 percent did not return because of price. This means open lines of communication in your center are very important. You also have to show your willingness to solve disputes quickly and fairly. Just as you talked to your staff about ways to work with new families, talk with them about ways to keep current families happy. How do you handle disputes with parents? How do you let them know about tuition increases? How do you move children to a new teacher or classroom in a way that is sensitive to parents' concerns? Use the ideas in the next section to help your staff think about ways to show families how much you appreciate them.

IDEA **101** *DAILY GREETINGS*

Families enter and leave through your doorway several hundred times each year and you may begin to take them for granted. Do you greet each parent and child every day? Think about how good it makes you feel when you walk into your doctor's office and the receptionist says to you, "Good morning, JoAnn. How are you today?" Everything you do to make your families feel more comfortable helps to cement the bond between you, even a simple hello and smile every day.

IDEA **102** *REGULAR NOTES HOME*

Keep the lines of communication open. At least once a week send home individual notes about each child's activities. For infants and young toddlers, these notes should go home each day, along with information about eating and sleeping. This can be a difficult task for teachers, so make it easier for them. Give them nice note paper on which to write their comments for parents. Provide time during the day for them to write. Give a workshop on appropriate comments. I have found that parents treasure these notes (not checklists!) especially if they leave their child in your care all day.

IDEA **103** **DAILY FEEDBACK**

Ask your teachers to give each parent positive feedback at the end of each day. This is especially important, and difficult timewise, in an all-day program. Working parents often feel they are missing their children's childhood and appreciate hearing about the little things that happen each day. The feedback can be very simple. "Carla really enjoyed finger painting with shaving cream today," or "Joshua is working on tying his shoes. Ask him to show you." On some trying days, it may simply be, "Jeremy's wearing such a cute shirt today." Providing this feedback helps to build a solid relationship between your families and your center.

IDEA **104** **WHEN A CHILD HAS A BAD DAY**

All children have bad days. There is an overwhelming desire for tired teachers to dump information about a child's bad day on parents when they pick them up. Teachers need to remember that the parent is tired too and still faces an entire evening with the family.

If the behavior is a one-time occurrence, there is usually no need to talk about it, unless the teacher can state the information in a positive way. "Linda seemed to have a hard day. She may need some time on your lap tonight to be rocked." If the problem is ongoing, schedule a special conference where everyone can talk calmly about how to solve the problem. Using this technique will go a long way toward building positive communications between parents and your staff.

Send greeting cards to let families know you are thinking about them. This encourages loyalty.

Always send a card when you learn of a family crisis. Send cards on happy occasions, too, such as new births or adoptions. You can also send birthday cards to each child at home. Some centers even include birthday cards for siblings.

Consider sending holiday cards to all your families. Christmas cards are the most common, but you can send them on other holidays when your card stands out. How about Thanksgiving cards that say thank you for choosing our center for your child? If you decide to send cards, be sensitive about the types of holidays your parents celebrate. It is inappropriate to send holiday cards to families who do not celebrate the holiday.

For many parents of toddlers, your center is their child's first group experience in child care. Many of these parents are concerned about making the right child care decision. To help ease their minds, host a brown bag lunch for these parents without the children. Before the luncheon, arrange to have your toddler room videotaped. Show this videotape of a typical day during the lunch. The tape can be a compilation of several days if you have someone who can edit a videotape. Use the tape as a springboard for conversations about their children. A special note: directors who use this idea run a video camera in the room for several days prior to the big taping day. They then encourage the staff in that room to look at the tape privately to become accustomed to having the camera present and seeing themselves on video.

You can also show this videotape during open houses or receptions (Idea #14), at your anniversary celebration (Idea #55) or to prospective parents during an enrollment visit.

IDEA  **107** **CALLING A PARENT AT WORK**

How many mornings have you seen a child walk into your center in tears with parents leaving and feeling distraught? If a child comes in unhappy, call the parent at home or work midmorning to say all is okay. Depending on the circumstances, you might even want to put the child on the phone.

IDEA **108** **MONTHLY NEWSLETTERS**

Send monthly letters or newsletters to all parents. Your teachers can write these newsletters for their own rooms, since you will be busy writing a different newsletter for prospective parents and community members (see Idea #13). Make arrangements to have each letter proofread before it is printed and distributed. In my experience I found that teachers not only enjoyed writing their own letters, they were much better at it than I was.

IDEA **10** **SUGGESTION BOX**

To encourage feedback from parents, try a parent suggestion box. And don't forget one for your employees. If employees have gripes that are not resolved, you can be sure their negative feelings will trickle down to parents. Both parents and employees often have great ideas for providing better customer service. Invite those comments and implement their suggestions.

When you receive a complaint, act on it immediately. Remember, 1=27. If there is nothing you can do, say so. If it is an anonymous complaint, paraphrase the issue on a piece of paper and respond in writing. Post the issue and your response on the parent or employee bulletin board. If you receive a suggestion about how you can better serve your families, respond to it as well. Post the suggestion on the board with an answer that tells parents and employees how you are implementing the idea.

Do not mount the suggestion boxes right outside your office. Neither parents nor employees will want to drop them off there. Put the suggestion boxes in locations where everyone can easily drop a note in without being seen.

If a parent is unhappy with someone in the center, is there someone else for the parent to talk to? Most parents know they can talk to the director if they are unhappy with a teacher, but what if the teacher is also the director? What if they are unhappy with the director? Having an anonymous suggestion box helps. A separate Parent Council or Advisory Group is another way to deal with problems. If you have a Parent Council or Advisory Group, let your parents know it exists. Encourage them to contact the council or group when they have problems they can't bring to you. Include information about the Parent Council or Advisory Group in your enrollment packet. Be sure they know how to contact representatives.

If you are an owner, you might want to write a welcome letter at the beginning of the parent handbook. In the letter, list your telephone number and invite parents to call you if they have questions or concerns.

IDEA **11** **WHEN A PARENT LEAVES**

Talk with every parent who leaves your program and let them know they are welcome back at any time. Keep them on your mailing list. Let them know about new programs in your center or new teachers in their child's age group. Parents often do not realize how good your program is until they go to another center. When you let them know they can return whenever they want, you relieve them of their embarrassment when their other arrangements fall through. Directors who use this approach report a surprisingly high percentage of parents who return.

IDEA **112** *EXIT INTERVIEWS*

Exit interviews give you the opportunity to learn the reasons why families leave your program. During an exit interview, parents will often reveal their true feelings, especially if they left because they were unhappy with some aspect of your program.

To be effective, exit interviews should be conducted within three to five days after the family leaves. The interview can consist of a telephone conversation or a written questionnaire. To encourage honesty, have telephone interviews conducted by someone outside your center and have written questionnaires returned to someone other than the director. Track the information you receive. If you see patterns in the responses, implement needed changes.

5

PUTTING IT ALL TOGETHER:
DEVELOPING AN ACTION PLAN

You have picked out the ideas you like and you are ready to go. Wait! You still need a road map, a guide to keep you on the path.

Your road map, or action plan, doesn't need to be long or complicated. Its purpose is to make sure you spend your time and money where it makes the most sense. I find this approach appealing, because as a director I never seemed to have enough time or money.

After developing this simple road map, you will find it much easier to respond to the sales people who call you about advertising in their publications or circulars. You simply reach in your desk, get out your road map and see if the proposed advertisement fits in with your strategy and your budget. If it fits, go for it. If not, thank the sales persons and let them be on their way.

"But," you say, "I don't have time to develop an action plan."

I understand. Your time is scarce, so let's keep it simple. Jay Conrad Levinson has developed an easy approach to action plans. He calls it a "seven-sentence marketing plan."* I have developed and reviewed action plans for many years and this approach is the best I have ever seen. With his permission, I am reproducing it for you with some minor alterations. The success of this approach is living proof that long, intimidating action plans aren't necessary for your center's success.

Here are the seven sentences for your road map. I have also included an example.

1. One sentence tells the purpose of your marketing.

"The purpose of ABC Preschool's marketing is to build enrollment in the toddler rooms."

2. One sentence tells how this purpose will be achieved, focusing on the benefits of your program.

"We will achieve this by focusing on our low staff-child ratios (our ability to give each child one-on-one attention) and our inviting classroom environment (a place where children feel at home)."

3. One sentence defines your target audience.

"Our target audience is middle-income, working parents who live within a three-mile radius of our center."

4. One sentence tells about your competitive niche (what makes you different from your competitors) in the market.

"ABC Preschool's niche is our affordable, high quality early childhood program for working parents."

5. One sentence gives your identity.

"We will portray ourselves as warm, friendly and knowledgeable about parents and families issues, which we will show by being visible in the community, by being warm and caring with families when we talk to them on the telephone, by having a plan to help each family enter our center with the least possible trauma to the child and by maintaining daily communication with our parents about their children."

6. One sentence describes your proposed marketing vehicles.

"The marketing vehicles we will use include writing and distributing a new community newsletter, hosting bimonthly parenting workshops for our families and the neighborhood, using a new Yellow Pages ad that focuses on our warm and caring approach to children, developing a special brochure for new parents, purchasing "How to Choose Infant and Toddler Care" and "Separation" pamphlets and distributing them in the community through "Take One" boxes and sending them to parents when they call us about our program, becoming accredited by the National Academy of Early Childhood Programs, encouraging our current parents to make referrals by letting them know about openings in our toddler rooms, and providing training to staff members about how to answer the telephone."

7. One sentence describes your marketing budget.

"We will set aside two percent of our projected gross income to use for building enrollment."

See how easy that is? Even those of us without a business background can write seven sentences about how we want to build enrollment. You might want to add some attachments, such as several pages of notes or documentation, a calendar or a more detailed budget. The key to your successful implementation, nevertheless, is your seven-sentence plan. After you write it, be sure you review it often to make any necessary adjustments.

* For other guerrilla marketing tools by Jay Conrad Levinson, contact Guerrilla Marketing International at 1-800-748-6444.

A FINAL NOTE

Be realistic! Don't feel that you need to do everything at once. Start by trying out one new idea a month. Track your enrollments to see if an idea is successful. If an idea or event is not, ask staff and parents you trust if it is worth trying again. Remember to give an idea time to work. Building enrollment takes time.

Be patient! Marketing usually doesn't generate instant results. People need to hear your message many, many times before they hear and respond to it. This means you need to be out in the community helping people hear and remember your name. They will become familiar with your name through the marketing ideas you implement from this book.

Remain committed! It's often difficult to stay committed to "marketing" – after all, aren't we in this profession because we are committed to children? Look at it this way. Building enrollment helps you offer better services to children. You already know this intuitively when working with your program's budget. If each classroom in your school is short by two or three children, you're missing out on lots of income. If you were at capacity in each of those rooms, you would have extra money to purchase equipment or supplies, buy a computer, or give your teachers a raise. But to get those extra enrollments, and therefore offer those extras to your children, you need to stay committed to your marketing efforts over the long run.

Do this all year round, especially when your program is full. The tendency is to wait until enrollment is down to start marketing and promoting your center. If this has happened to you, it certainly is not too late to start. Then don't stop once you are full. Plan promotional activities a little at a time, spread throughout the year. It will remain fun and won't become a burden.

Delegate! As you read these ideas, think about how staff members in your program can become involved. For example, if you organize a children's art show at a bank, ask teachers to mount the pictures on an attractive backing. If you write a community newsletter, ask staff for ideas and stories. When all staff members are involved with promoting your program, everyone feels proud of being a part of the team.

Have fun! If you really believe that you offer the best program for children – and I know you do, or you wouldn't be spending so much of your time and energy in your center – you will find it is rewarding and fun to let people know that your center is a great place for children.

APPENDICES

APPENDICES

PARENT INQUIRY

Date _____

Parent Name _____

Address _____

_____

Home Phone _____

Work Phone _____

Child(ren)'s Name _____ Age _____

_____ Age _____

Schedule: (circle one)   a.m.   p.m.   all day

Number of days/weeks _____

Price quoted _____

Desired start date _____

Program Needs/Desires

_____

_____

_____

_____

_____

_____

_____

_____

_____

Visit Scheduled: Date _____

Time _____

Date	Type of Follow-up
_____	Brochure mailed
_____	Follow-up telephone call
_____	Invitation to open house
_____	_____
_____	_____
_____	_____

Comments _____

_____

_____

_____

_____

_____

_____ Deposit received   Amount $_____

_____ Enrollment materials sent

_____ Completed enrollment materials received

_____ Starting date

_____ Teacher notified

_____ Assigned Classroom

Developed by The Creative Planning Group

WORKSHEET: BENEFITS AND FEATURES

In Idea #75 in the Telephone Tips section of this book, I discussed the important difference between the benefits and features of your program. This worksheet will help you develop benefits statements about your school. First, re-read Idea #75. Then list the key features of your program in one column, and then restate them as benefits in the other column.

Remember, a benefit focuses on what the family (parent or child) receives; a feature describes a service you offer or a fact about your program. When you are talking with parents, use phrases about your features to support your benefits statements.

HINT: Start a benefits phrase with the words "You," "Your child," or "Your family." A phrase about features will begin with "Our center," "We," "I" or "His teacher."

FEATURE	BENEFIT
Example: *"We have low* *staff/child ratios.*	*"Your toddler will receive* *lots of individualized,* *one-on-one attention* *from his teachers."*

FEATURE

BENEFIT

WORKSHEET: SEVEN-SENTENCE ACTION PLAN

Use this worksheet to develop your own seven-sentence action plan. You may want to refer to the example listed in Chapter 5. Remember, you can attach as much documentation to this action plan as you want.

1. One sentence tells the purpose of your marketing.

2. One sentence tell how this purpose will be achieved, focusing on the benefits of your program.

3. One sentence defines your target audience.

4. One sentence tells about your competitive niche (what makes you different from your competitors) in the market.

5. One sentence gives your identity.

6. One sentence describes your proposed marketing vehicles.

7. One sentence describes your marketing budget.

INDEX

ORDER FORM

101 Ways to Build Enrollment in Your Early Childhood Program makes a great gift for a friend or colleague. Send a copy to someone who has just become a new director, to a friend who recently changed to a new center, to a student or aspiring director. It is an affordable Christmas gift too!

No director should be without *101 Ways to Build Enrollment!* Send for extra copies today.

Name _____

Program Name _____

Address _____

City _____ State _____ Zip _____

Please send _____ copies of

101 Ways to Build Enrollment @ $12.95 each. $_____

Sales tax* $_____

Postage/handling** $_____

TOTAL ENCLOSED $_____

Please make checks payable to **CPG Publishing Company**

* Arizona residents add 6.7%
** $2.75 for the first book and 50 cents for each additional book

If this is gift, would you like us to send it directly? We will enclose a FREE gift card for you! _____ Yes

Gift recipient's name _____

Program Name _____

Address _____

City _____ State _____ Zip _____

What would you like us to say on the card?

_____

_____

Mail to: CPG Publishing Company, P.O. Box 50062,
Phoenix, AZ 85076 1-800-578-5549

ORDER FORM

101 Ways to Build Enrollment in Your Early Childhood Program makes a great gift for a friend or colleague. Send a copy to someone who has just become a new director, to a friend who recently changed to a new center, to a student or aspiring director. It is an affordable Christmas gift too!

No director should be without *101 Ways to Build Enrollment!* Send for extra copies today.

Name _____

Program Name _____

Address _____

City _____ State _____ Zip _____

Please send _____ copies of

101 Ways to Build Enrollment @ $12.95 each. $_____

Sales tax* $_____

Postage/handling** $_____

TOTAL ENCLOSED $_____

Please make checks payable to **CPG Publishing Company**

* Arizona residents add 6.7%
** $2.75 for the first book and 50 cents for each additional book

If this is gift, would you like us to send it directly? We will enclose a FREE gift card for you!   _____ Yes

Gift recipient's name _____

Program Name _____

Address _____

City _____ State _____ Zip _____

What would you like us to say on the card?

_____

_____

Mail to: CPG Publishing Company, P.O. Box 50062,
Phoenix, AZ 85076 1-800-578-5549

HOW _YOU_ HAVE BUILT ENROLLMENT
IN YOUR PROGRAM

Are you interested in sharing ideas that have worked for you? They don't need to be fancy (the best ideas usually aren't!). If you send me an idea for building enrollment that I include in my next book, I'll send you $10 and will mention your name and the name of your program, if you wish.

You idea can be an advertising idea, a way to say thank you to parents for a referral, a way to encourage referrals, ways that you reach out to the community, brochure ideas, a catch business card or anything else you do.

Use the back or additional sheets if you need more room or if you have additional ideas. You can send more than one idea.

An idea for building enrollment that worked for me:

_____

_____

_____

_____

_____

_____

_____

_____

_____

Your Name _____

Program Name _____

Address _____

City _____ State _____ Zip _____

If I use your example in the book, may I use your name? _____ yes _____ no

Mail to: Ellen Orton Montanari
　　　　c/o CPG Publishing Company
　　　　P.O. Box 50062, Phoenix, AZ 85076

HOW _YOU_ HAVE BUILT ENROLLMENT
IN YOUR PROGRAM

Are you interested in sharing ideas that have worked for you? They don't need to be fancy (the best ideas usually aren't!). If you send me an idea for building enrollment that I include in my next book, I'll send you $10 and will mention your name and the name of your program, if you wish.

You idea can be an advertising idea, a way to say thank you to parents for a referral, a way to encourage referrals, ways that you reach out to the community, brochure ideas, a catch business card or anything else you do.

Use the back or additional sheets if you need more room or if you have additional ideas. You can send more than one idea.

An idea for building enrollment that worked for me:

_____

_____

_____

_____

_____

_____

_____

_____

_____

_____

Your Name _____

Program Name _____

Address _____

City _____ State _____ Zip _____

If I use your example in the book, may I use your name? _____ yes _____ no

Mail to: Ellen Orton Montanari
        c/o CPG Publishing Company
        P.O. Box 50062, Phoenix, AZ 85076